Heaven, Healing, & Pristine Health Orbs & Angelic Guidance to Heal Your Mind, Body, & Spirit

DIANA ALBA

CTN, CHom, CNC, CT, RM, ATP®, Artist, Medical Intuitive, Psychic Medium

Copyright © 2015 Diana L. Alba

All rights reserved.

ISBN: 0692371842
ISBN-13: 978-0692371848

DEDICATION

This book is dedicated to God, Source, Divine, Angels, Orbs, Spirit Guides, and to my loved ones who have crossed over into their new assignment. Their constant presence is with me and has always been with me in my journey. And to everyone who believes in miracles, to my husband Emilio, my children Vannessa, Jessica, Amanda, Glenn, Keith, and to our grandchildren Grace, Sean, Brooke, and Eliza.

May all of your vibrations continue to soar.

Introduction

So what is an Orb?

An Orb is an energetic physical manifestation of Angels, Guides, Spirit, and DLO's (dead loved ones). Orbs are commonly experienced as a circle or sphere of light. Orbs come in many shapes, sizes, and colors; including spiraling flashes of brilliant light, lacey mists, or luminescent glowing tubes of energy. An Orb is a beautiful and gentle sign from Heaven that we are never alone.

Who Am I?

I am a Traditional Naturopath, Classical Homeopath, Certified Thermographer, qEEG -- Brain NeuroIntegration Specialist, Certified Nutritional Consultant, Reiki Master, Angel Therapy Practitioner®, Author, Artist, Medical Intuitive, and Psychic Medium.

For almost twenty years I have seen thousands of people for numerous reasons. Issues have ranged from emotional trauma, anxiety, depression, IBS, insomnia, high blood pressure, diabetes, chronic fatigue, hormone imbalances, grief, loss of a loved one, ADD/ADHD, OCD, chronic pain, general health and wellness, eczema and skin rashes, to channeling messages from departed loved ones, Spirt, and Angels.

Over the years I have been asked many times how I know what I know. I answer by explaining that I am constantly continuing my education, that I have an excellent memory, and that my intuitive abilities began when I was a child. I also share a few pictures of my "sparklers" and Orbs.

My childhood "sparklers" turned out to be Angels, and they encouraged/nudged me to share their photos and my experiences with others in the form of this book. I finally agreed, in spite of my self-doubt and worry that people would think I was wackadoodle. So many Angels show up in several pictures that it looks like a *Star Trek* scene from outer space! When someone says "prove it" or "show me a picture and then I will believe it"...you now have some pictures of my friends!

When you hear someone say "The most horrific thing just

happened to me. It has been making me sick to my stomach. I am getting hives, and now I am giving up," this shows how our mind, body, and spirit really are connected. I believe that when these three areas are addressed simultaneously, we can restore our joy, health, and purpose.

My approach centers on these three things, Mind, Body, and Spirit … a "Trinity."

Our "Mind" is our ego. Our minds are made up of thoughts, judgements, personality, Divine energy, and choice/free will.

Our "Body" is our physical vessel and our incredible "sensory" gift on Earth. Our physical bodies are subject to our joy, stress, choices, environment, genetics, nutrition, injury, and miracles. As our Mind believes, our Body can achieve.

Our "Spirit" is our soul. Our Spirit is our whole and complete connection to God, Source, Divine. We are all one; we are all blessed. Our spirit is the Divine Energy that imbues all living souls.

We have the ability to make choices with our *Mind*. We have the ability to heal our *Body*. We have the ability to communicate with *Spirit*. These are gifts we are born with.

My goal is to share my knowledge, life experiences, and set you free with the tools to help guide you in your journey of self-healing.

CONTENTS

	Dedication	
	Introduction	i
	Part 1	
1	How This All Started	1
2	God, Angels, & Orbs	16
	Archangel Michael	19
	Archangel Gabriel	23
	Archangel Raphael	29
	Archangel Uriel	34
	Archangel Chamuel	39
	Archangel Metatron	45
	Archangel Sandalphon	53
	Archangel Ariel	57
	Archangel Jophiel	62
	Archangel Jeremiel	76
	Archangel Zadkiel	81
	Archangel Azrael	88
	My Guides	92

Part 2

3	Human Angels	101
4	Intention & Energy Healing	110
5	Chakras, Common Maladies, Simple Steps for Self-Healing	120
6	Space Clearing – My $25 Lesson	133
7	Meditation & Prayer	143
8	Coincidence, Serendipity, Nudges, Smackdowns, & Fate	148
9	Putting It All Together	158
10	Focused Intention	165
	About The Author	169
	Acknowledgements	170

1 HOW THIS ALL STARTED

BAZINGA....I was born....with the umbilical cord wrapped snuggly around my neck and a lovely blue tinge to my face. It was the perfect time to get started with this thing called life.

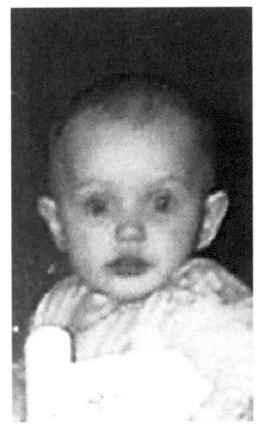

My arrival happened in 1960 on a military base in Charleston, South Carolina. Instant dry milk, Karo corn syrup, and water were considered an excellent mixture for baby formula. I still have the recipe card from the base hospital. Dwight D. Eisenhower was the president, the Beatles invaded the United States, Medicare began, the outdoor concert in Woodstock, NY, was held, Astronaut Neil Armstrong walked on the moon, John F. Kennedy, Malcolm X, Martin Luther King, Jr., and Senator Robert Kennedy were all assassinated. Miniskirts, drugs, free love, the Monkees, my name...a song called "Diana," by Paul Anka (released in 1957 about his crush on his babysitter), and of course, Viet Nam. Televisions were a luxury that had rabbit ear antennas plus knobs to turn the channels. No one had a cell phone, except for the cool gadgets they had on the Starship *Enterprise* -- remember *Star Trek*? Yes, yes, yes, I was in love with Spock as a child. And now I am in love with Sheldon from *The Big Bang Theory*. The 1960s -- what a great time to show up.

From the time of my birth until about the age of three I was mostly working on building the neural connections needed for my 100 billion brain cells. I ate, slept, puttered around, drank blackberry brandy from a bottle, and wanted to avoid being touched or held by

Chapter 1 How this all started

anyone. By the age of three, I knew something was very different about me.

<u>Options other than blackberry brandy in a bottle for sleep:</u>
- Hyland's Homeopathic Calming Tablets OTC
- Lullaby with Hemi-Sync® CDs for Children (on line)

Memory is an interesting thing. How the brain stores memory is interesting as well. What makes one person recall every detail of every day in their life, like Marilu Henner? I believe it is a gift from above. I too was blessed with a good memory. When I look at something or read something that interests me, it becomes a picture in my head, a movie in my mind that I can recall and review upon my request. One such memory that I have not forgotten: I was three years old, peeking around the hallway corner watching the black-and-white television. I was supposed to be in bed. The evening news was replaying the funeral procession of President John F. Kennedy. I felt the devastation in Walter Cronkite's voice. The wails of the people filmed in the background. There is little concept of death for the average three-year-old. After watching for a while I went back down the hall and crawled into my bed. I had such a resounding feeling of despair, confusion, and emptiness. What would happen to the two children shown on the news that night? They looked so blank, and they felt sad to me. Little did I know that my own "Lone Wolf Era of Self-Preservation" was about to start in full force.

Time moves on and now I am between four and six years old. I have very vivid memories of this time period. We had already moved from South Carolina to several other places in the country: Phillips, Wisconsin; Cicero, Illinois; and Missoula, Montana. I very much enjoyed Montana. We lived in the middle of nowhere, much like the scenes from the movie *A River Runs Through It*. I so loved to go to the river's edge and pull out worms, snail shells, rocks, and then grab myself a handful of mud. These materials made excellent wrappings

Chapter 1 How this all started

for my beautiful sun-dried foot coverings. First you put the mud on the tops of your feet. Then you add the earthly decorations, let them dry in the sun, listen to the wind, feel the warmth, and see the sparklers in the air. Then presto, you have an amazing spa day. I have subsequently found a better option than river mud, worms, rocks, and snail shells for topical spa applications.

- Volcanic sulfur mud, hand gathered from a volcano in Barbados
- Over-the-counter plain mud masks from any local store (better option)

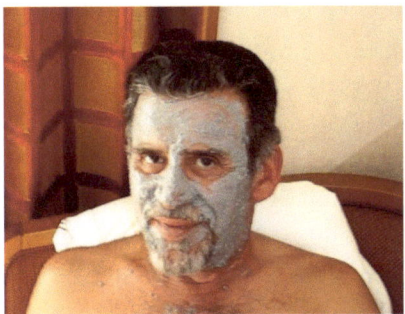 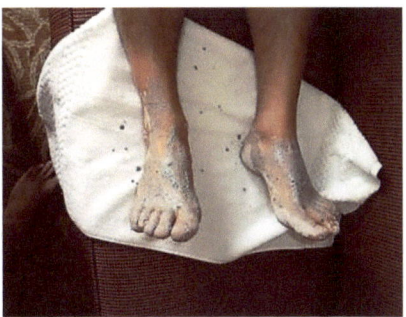

Barbados sulphur on my husband's face and feet; he is my guinea pig.

Me in Montana, in my happy place, in the mud.

The sparklers in the air in Montana made me quite delighted. Have you ever looked at or through the space within the air? You can see sparklers too.

This may sound wackadoodle, but it is true. If you are looking at a tree, relax your eyes, then look through the air between the trees and your eyes. You'll see the sparklers, similar to seeing dust particles moving through the air during a lazy morning in bed. Or like watching somebody shake out a rug in the sunrays. But I am not talking about dirty-rug dust particles in the air, I am talking about energy particles, and how you can see them if you just relax your eyes. Just as if you are trying to see the dust. I could see the sparklers, flashes, and flares of light from an

Chapter 1 How this all started

early age. I thought everyone saw them. Talking about them to anyone caused people to squint at me as though I was missing brain tissue, or that I was Jon Lovitz (the Liar) from *Saturday Night Live*; so I simply stopped talking about it.

One night in Montana my three siblings and I did not want to settle down and go to sleep. Subsequently we children were sent outside to stand in the cold, wearing just our underwear, and face the Yuckies. The Yuckies were some kind of horrible creatures that would tear us up, kill us, and then eat us….like Bigfoot or mountain lions, or worse.

We hid from the moonlight by standing against the wall of the house, in the shadows, shivering. I prayed and looked for the sparklers. Lucky for me, my sparklers were there. This kept me focused and not afraid as the time passed slowly. Eventually, our parents let us back in the house. In my opinion, this was not a cool way to punish small children for wanting to stay awake. When I finally got into my bed I thanked my sparklers for keeping me safe.

I was reading the comics and telling time by the age of four. So eventually, off to kindergarten I went. Several short weeks later, I was taken out of school. The school wanted to put me in first or second grade, beyond an older sibling. That did not sit well with our parents, so I was kept at home instead. This didn't bother me at all. I just thought it was silly, and continued to read the newspaper, comics, and announce the time all day long. I tried to show them that I was smart. They were not impressed.

Have any of you had an outhouse? I did. Have any of you taken your baths in a metal washtub? I did, for years. We were living in Phillips, Wisconsin. I was in first grade. There was a rope tied from the front of the house all the way to the outhouse door, just in case you got lost on your way in the dark or in the snow. This is when I saw my first human spirit-ghost.

I had returned from the outhouse, scared out of my pants

because I thought someone or something was out in the woods with me. I sat on my bed and looked up the narrow staircase leading to an attic in this very small cottage. We were not allowed to go up the rickety stairs to the attic. That evening I felt a very cold breeze and saw an airy, but dense, white/gray mist on those rickety wooden stairs. It looked like a woman in a long cotton night gown. This scared the crap out of me. I ran to my parents' sleeping area and was told to go back to bed. As I crept back to my bed, she followed me around the corner and then disappeared into the tattered, plaster-coated wood-slat wall. My little heart was pounding out of my chest as I burrowed under the covers and prayed that she would not hurt me. She was my first ghost. She did not "feel" like a gentle or happy person, not like the sparklers of light I was used to. I was not sure if tucking the blanket all the way around me, under me, and praying could save me from her cold gray energy.

Apparently it worked, as I am still here.

My parents had a very tough marriage, and a total of four children at this point. Together, not together, yelling, screaming, and stupid violence. I guess they were doing the best they could with what they had. Lots of crummy times. I just got used to it and went about my business.

I am fourteen months old with two pheasant's for dinner, oh my!

Chapter 1 How this all started

Farmington, Minnesota was another stop in my childhood travels. I spent part of my time during third grade in the fifth grade math class. I sat in the back row and could barely see the front of the classroom. When I finished my math assignments I drew on my extra paper. One day when I was bored, I drew a horse, pulled out some crayons, and colored it red and brown. I was pleased with my creation. I turned in my math paper and my horse picture to my teacher. She gaped at me as if I had two heads. I thought I was in trouble or that my "art" was terrible. Nope, she took my drawing to the principal and the next thing I knew my drawing had earned me a blue ribbon and a place in the trophy case at the school. So nice. That inspired me to draw on everything. I would close my eyes and imagine the most beautiful horse and what the jaw, ears, legs, and eyes were doing. I would open my eyes to find that I always drew the same horse. I still do today. I only have a few pictures of myself as a kid. Check out my bee-stung face on this amazing carousel horse. So happy.

I spent much of my time in the fields, the forest, exploring ponds, streams, and whatever else I could find or fit my body into. One day in the cornfield, age nine, I found what I thought was a *huge*, square concrete swimming pool, above ground. It was partially filled with stinky green and brown water. I saw a large jackrabbit sitting

Chapter 1 How this all started

under a pile of broken cornstalks. He was simply watching me. I watched him awhile as well. I then decided I needed a pet. I talked to the rabbit as I walked around the stinky concrete pool, getting closer and closer. In an instant I opened my jacket and pounced on him like a flying squirrel. Oh my gosh, it worked. I had caught myself a new pet rabbit, but how could I stand up and not drop him? I pondered this as he wiggled to get free. Careful not to put all of my weight on him, I made a cocoon shape with my body and protected him with my jacket. I must have been on the ground for *quite some time*, until we both finally relaxed and waited to see what I would do next.

I heard a loud rumbling and could feel it with my body on the ground. Then the noise and vibration stopped. It was a corn combine tractor. An old farmer got out and walked up to me as I lay on the ground in that weird position. He asked me if I was okay and what I was doing way out in the cornfield by myself. From my protective military commando position on the ground, I told him I had found a swimming pool and that I had caught a rabbit. He said the swimming pool had been a water trough for cattle in the past, but the water was now "contaminated," so to stay away from it. I learned a new word. It became my favorite word for quite a while ... "CONTAMINATED." He walked over to me and reached down to grab the back of my jacket to stand me up. That is when he saw my rabbit's legs sticking out from under me. He acknowledged that I had indeed caught a jackrabbit and that I should get up carefully and let him go. I said no. I told him I wanted to bring him home because nobody would believe me, and my rabbit was probably afraid and lost in the cornfield. He agreed. He told me to hang on to his hind legs and feet with both of my hands and that he would hold the rabbit's head and front legs as I stood up. Wow, it worked! Now we were both standing up holding this rabbit. I hung on really well as this old farmer zipped up my jacket with the rabbit inside. He hesitated a moment and then gave me a weird look. He told me to make sure not to let go of the rabbit's hind legs until I had someone to help me. I walked the long way home from the cornfield, happy as a clam with my new furry friend in my coat.

When I reached the back of the farmhouse I started yelling for someone to open the door. I had to go up several concrete steps to get to the old wooden screen door. How was I supposed to open it with no hands? My mother came to the door and saw I had something alive in my jacket. She told me that I could not bring whatever it was into the house. She would not open the door. So I decided to open the door myself, which meant taking one of my hands off of my new friend. That was a huge mistake. My rabbit was very smart and took this opportunity to kick with all of his might. That is what jackrabbits do. I felt burning on my chest and neck as I started to bleed. My skin got ripped to pieces from his sharp nails while he was kicking and squirming to get free. He took off and disappeared back into that cornfield. Game over, ten points for my rabbit, zero points for me.

Everyone is born with unique gifts and innate intuition or "senses". If a young child declares they can *hear* and *see* music in their head and then bangs out a tune by Mozart; we scream, *"It's a miracle"*. There are names for these types of gifts, and these gifts come from extra sensory awareness.

Our world is made up of energy and vibrations. Some we can readily see, feel, and hear, like lightning. Many things are not as easily comprehended as lightning, but that doesn't mean they are not real. Let's say you were thinking about asking someone to tea. You punch in the number into your cell phone from Colorado to call the Queen of England. Assuming she answers her phone, she will be able to hear your voice in a New York second. She heard and felt her cell phone ringing and vibrating, so she answered it, thus making the connection. You start to blow air through a few flaps of tissue (vocal cords) to create a frequency (your voice) into your cell phone. How did your voice travel across the pond so quickly? Can you see it? No. Can you hear it? Yes. If the person you called is happy or depressed, can you feel it? Yes. If you ask a question and get silence…you probably know the answer before you hear it…don't you!

We can feel others' energy. Consider when a person or stranger gives you bad vibes or a prickly feeling. When a person or stranger has a good vibe you feel happy tingles. When you feel something in your body physically, that is clairsentience. When you hear something in your mind, or outside of your mind, that is clairaudience.

Chapter 1 How this all started

A few definitions for you:

- The sense of feeling *something physically* is called **Clairsentience**. You get a feeling as though you are choking, can't breathe, or like you just got hit in the head, but none of these things are actually happening to you.
- The sense of *clear seeing* is called **Clairvoyance**. This is the ability to gain information about an object, person, location, or physical event through means other than the known senses, as in Mediumship.
- The sense of *clear hearing/listening* outside of what others can hear is called **Clairaudience**. You hear someone yell, "stop the car! Don't go through that intersection," and you are by yourself. Then a truck runs a red light right in front of you.
- The sense of *clear tasting* is called **Clairgustiance.** You taste pineapple, meatloaf, boysenberries, blood, saltwater, etc., and you don't have it in your mouth.
- The sense of *clear smelling* is called **Clairalience**. You smell cigar smoke, you are not smoking a cigar, and you are the only one home.
- The sense of *clear* k*nowing* a fact you know nothing about is called **Claircognizance**. This is the ability to know something without a physical explanation as to why or how you know it, and you are correct.
- The sense of *precognition* is called being **Psychic**. This is the ability to acquire the knowledge of future events or information that cannot be deduced from currently available or normally attained sense-based information.
- The ability to *communicate messages* and

information to the living from spirits, angels, ascended masters, guides, lost loved ones, or Source, is called **Mediumship**. A medium has psychic and channeling abilities, but not all psychics function as or have the abilities of mediums.

- The ability called **Channeling** means that the channeler goes into a trance, meditative state, or "leaves their body". They allow an entity to borrow their body and then speak through them, relaying information and/or guidance about the past, present, or future.

We are born with five basic senses: vision, hearing, smell, taste, and touch. We also have a sixth sense I call *"intuitive communication,"* or as more commonly known, ESP, *extrasensory perception.*

Can a person read or write with their eyes closed? Most people immediately answer *"No way."* But, of course they can, it is called *Braille.* In 1824, a blind teenager named Louis Braille developed a code of dots for the French alphabet using embossed paper. His genius proved that with practice our brains can read through touch.

All of our senses can be vastly improved or heightened through practice and focused intention. As a young child I was aware of this *"extra sense"* and believed that everyone knew about their *"extra sense."* Since I had very little desire to talk to people, I spent much of my free time having conversations in my mind with God or my Sparklers. Often when I asked a question in my mind the answer would pop into my head in the form of a picture or words. If the answer didn't eventually pop into my head, it would not be long before I was given a *"sign."* The *"sign"* could be as simple as overhearing a related conversation which held the answer. Other times I would open a book to a random page and there was my answer.

These question and answer sessions with heaven became a fun game for me. I would think up a question, imagine the answer, and wait to see if I was right. The more I played this game the more accurate my answers became.

As I grew up I realized that answers were available at any time, like radio waves in the air. We are all surrounded by radio waves, yet we can't hear the music unless we become a receiver and tune into a specific channel. If you want to listen to love songs on 101.1 FM you can't tune into 850 AM and expect to hear *"Muskrat Love."* Many years ago radios came with dials that had to be adjusted ever so slightly to find a station. Tuning in to ones' intuition or extrasensory perception is just like tuning an old radio. Think of the old TV show *Gilligan's Island.* Those seven shipwrecked folks tried for years to get off the island by using their portable AM radio receiver. The problem was nobody could hear them, so they spent many years trying to fix the broken transmitter. One way communication is not fun and rather lonely.

We are all born with a receiver and a transmitter. All we have to do to communicate clearly is practice tuning in and transmitting at the proper frequency. I have spent my whole life paying attention to small sensory ques and signs to develop and perfect my abilities. We can all do this through meditation, prayer, and quieting our mind. Ask your question, ask for an answer, and ask for an obvious sign. Send Heaven many thanks and sincere gratitude for the assistance. Be patient. Be aware of your surroundings and your thoughts. This is much like learning to play the piano. We start with learning the notes (frequencies). We progress to learning sheet music. We learn to play a simple song. We practice for hours and suddenly we can play the music by instinct, without sheet music, or looking at our hands. The notes start to flow intuitively and naturally.

We are all equipped with the tools to develop our *"clairs."* Like everything in life, practice makes perfect. Some people are born with an inner knowing of their life purpose. They practice thousands of hours to become a concert pianist. It is because of their hard work and dedication that we stand up amazed and applauding at the finish of their concerto.

Some people find their "gifts" later in life, in different areas, and excel beyond human belief. We all have a path, we all have special gifts, and we all find *"it"* in divine timing.

I have personally dropped my jaw in amazement at the gifts of a few people who have worked hard for many years to develop and perfect their abilities: my beautiful, heaven-sent friends Rebecca Rosen and Ariel Hardy, as well as my experiences with Anthony Williams, John Holland, James Van Praag, Tony Stockwell, and John Edwards. I encourage you to do an internet search and learn all about them.

Chapter 1 How this all started

There are many ways to develop your gifts. The first step is to be open to what you don't know and pay attention to little things, like a curious child. The phrase "that's impossible", needs to be forgotten. Throughout this book you will find descriptions, step by step instructions, and my personal experiences to guide you in your quest for healing and self-discovery. The second thing people need to do is to not give up, and practice, practice, practice. It may be rare for a four-year-old child to play a tune from Mozart; it is not rare to play that tune after you have practiced.

Did you know that when we record certain areas of the brain, we can now tell what object the person is thinking of? Isn't it crazy how science is proving what many scoffed at as hocus-pocus! Reading people's minds. Reading people's thoughts. Reading people's energy.

Before we had the abacus, math calculations took longer. Before we had the computer, math calculations took longer. If you lived in the time period of the abacus and said that a machine could do math faster, they would have put you in a cell and left you there. We are now recognizing the incredible capabilities of the machine called our brain, and the untapped gifts we were all born with.

When I was about eight years old life was pretty rough. Our parents had split up again, and we were bounced around from state to state, and city to city. During this time period we were living in the upper level of a pastor's house in Illinois, which they had converted into a very small one-bedroom apartment. It was quite sparse and it was furnished with very old, itchy furniture.

Going to yet another new school wasn't a whole lot of fun anymore. My teacher felt it was her place to announce to everyone that I was new, that my parents were getting a divorce, that I did not have pencils or paper, that I did not have a lunch with me, and so on. This teacher seemed to take great pleasure in making me feel like a charity case. I did not have fancy clothes like the other children and I did not know one soul in that room. The other kids watched me as if I was a zoo chimpanzee that had just shown up completely disheveled, expecting to join the party. You may remember the song "Harper Valley PTA" sang by Jeannie C. Riley. It was popular at the time. This song was about hypocrisy, judgement, and acting like you are better than someone else. Reality is that no one has a "perfect"

Chapter 1 How this all started

life. I wished I had enough courage to speak up and address this teacher, like the mom did in this song. My other favorite tune during this time was "D.I.V.O.R.C.E.", sang by Tammy Wynette. This song was about spelling *"sensitive"* words out loud during adult conversations to *"protect"* children. No one spelled words in front of me. I knew exactly what was going on. I memorized every word to those two songs and sang them constantly.

A few weeks into my latest school adventure in Illinois, I found that I had made myself two friends. One was a plump boy who sat behind me in class. He had curly white-blonde hair, pale skin, and red cheeks. He also had great lunches that he was happy to share with me. His metal Flintstone lunch box was enormous, somewhat like a briefcase. At the time a children's TV show called *Captain Kangaroo* featured a character called Mr. Green Jeans. They would demonstrate on the show what should go into a lunch bag for school. A banana, a sandwich, Ding-Dongs, a can of pop, chips, a candy bar…what a great lunch bag they put together! This boy had more treats than Mr. Green Jeans ever thought of putting into his lunch bag. He was a smart young nerd, and he called me "Dino".

He said that he really liked Dino the Dinosaur from *The Flintstones* and that I reminded him of his favorite character. I was super skinny, and I thought he looked more like Dino than I did. However, I decided this was not so bad. I rather liked having a nickname and sharing his lunch. He drew many pictures for me of Dino the Dinosaur; with hearts all over his drawings. My first admirer.

I liked another child in that class. She was in a wheelchair and had something really different about her face. She wore glasses, and her long brown curly hair hung down to cover one side of her face. She dressed very nicely. I never said anything to her about her face or her oddly shaped mouth. I never asked her why she was in a wheelchair. One day she casually explained her situation. She said when she was crawling around as a baby; she liked to chew on things. She had chewed on a lamp cord and was electrocuted. Her mouth and face were burned. She was left with nerve damage that made it hard for her to walk or use her hand. She didn't even blink an eye when she told me this. How could someone be so happy and kind after such a horrific event? She was so sweet. I couldn't understand why other kids did not befriend her as well.

Chapter 1 How this all started

It had been about two months since we moved there, and I had finally adjusted to my new reality. I knew my way home and didn't get lost anymore. I had a pretty good setup for school lunch, and I had a nickname.

One afternoon the teacher announced to the class that I was leaving. *What?* The other shoe dropped, yet again. She gave me a manila envelope with my school records in it and told me to bring it home with me. She walked me to the classroom door and said goodbye. I wanted to cry right then, but I didn't. I started my walk home, feeling confused, scared, depressed, and unwanted.

When I got into the apartment nobody was there, as usual. I lay face down on my bed and started to sob. I begged God to just let me die and to take me, as I had done many times before. Apparently God had other plans, as this day was going to turn out different.

I felt the warmth of the sun on me and I could see a bright light. How could that be? The room was dark, and my face was buried in my pillow, my eyes closed. I looked up from the pillow and saw that the room was filled with golden, white, and silver sparkling rays of light. I felt as if I had floated out of my body and was being suspended in midair. A voice from the light told me not to be afraid and that everything would be okay. I felt such a sense of calm and peacefulness. The next thing I knew, I was sitting up on the side of the bed. I was not crying anymore. I was not sad.

It took me a few minutes to come to grips with what had just happened. Then I realized that I had just seen the biggest sparkler I had ever seen, and it spoke to me. I felt safe and perfectly content. Incredible. I got up and went outside to my favorite blackberry bush. I ate berries until I was no longer hungry. The sun was warm and the grass was soft. My life was going to be okay. I was not alone. I realized that I would always have my "sparkler friends," as they had never left me. When their "boss" filled that dark room with love and light, I felt like I was home. That day, that moment, those words, changed my life forever.

I knew who my *"friendly sparklers"* were and that they were *real*. I knew they heard me and I could understand them. Everything really was going to be okay.

People say that you will know when you have a true friend, because they always show up for you. Many people have amazing pictures of themselves with their friends. Many people have taken

Chapter 1 How this all started

pictures of their friends doing incredible things. I have these types of pictures too.

I've never said I had a "normal" life. I've never claimed to be a "normal" person. Remember, I'm still the gal with a crush on Spock and Sheldon. I so, so, love the those boys!

Having grown up as a "lone wolf" created oodles of solitary time and the opportunity to meet some pretty cool dudes. Some of my friends and family may look a little different than what you might expect. Friends and family come in all different shapes and sizes, especially mine. I would like to share some pictures and introduce you to several of my closest buds.

Oh, and yes, I believe in Angels.

2 GOD, ANGELS, & ORBS

Most of us have been taught that we can talk to God through prayer, meditation, or thoughts. I agree. I talk to God every day, several times a day. To me, as an example: God is the King, and Angels are the Knights of the Round Table. When the King gets a request from one of his people, he takes action. He either responds himself or he sends one of his knights. Angels are like the knights and are Gods helpers.

How do you know who is who? The King usually wears a crown and a magnificent robe. The knights wear armor and a smaller cape. This is pretty basic stuff. We know "who is who" by relying on our past experiences and our senses.

Assume that you are wearing a blindfold and I want you to identify something by using your remaining senses. I hold a bowl of hot chili under your nose. You would know immediately that it was hot, because you felt the warmth and you would know it was chili by the way it smelled. You would "see" a bowel of hot chili in your mind, and you would be correct.

If you were invited to go to a party with a friend and you didn't know the host, you would probably ask several questions to help you identify the correct person. Your friend would then describe the party host in great detail, right down to the mole on their face. If I say "super model" and "mole," you think Cindy Crawford. If I say "peanuts" and "president," you think Jimmy Carter.

Identifying someone by their face is easy. Identifying someone from a distance is harder. What if you saw someone in a crowd that you thought you knew but you weren't sure? You might go over to them and ask, "Don't I know you?" They may look different, but they are still your friend.

We expect Angels or Spirit to look a certain way based on what we have been taught. This section is to share how I see, sense, and feel my "sparklers" from heaven. Angels can look like traditionally portrayed angels. Angels may look like a hazy mist, circles of light (Orbs), spheres, or flashes. They can also appear just like us. Loved ones in heaven appear similar, but with a different "texture." We often feel like we know them when we "see/sense" them. Their luminosity/texture is familiar and we are not afraid.

Let's say you are holding a rose. Close your eyes so you cannot see. Does this mean the rose has disappeared? Of course not. You are touching the rose, smelling the rose, seeing the rose in your mind, and feeling pure joy from the experience. If someone asked you to close your eyes and quickly pluck a petal you could immediately and accurately respond. If you were asked to perform this exercise numerous times, you might win a *Guinness Book of World Records* award for the fastest blind rose petal plucker. Why? Because you instinctively knew what to do and could see it in your mind.

God, angels, orbs, spirit, departed loved ones, and all of heavens miracles can be felt, seen, and experienced while we are here on Earth. We all have guides and Angels to encourage, help, and inspire us. Start looking for synchronicities in your life…someone is probably trying to give you a message. If your mother tells you three times to put your dishes in the sink, you eventually do it. If you see three wilted plants one day, don't you go home and water your own plants? The message can be anything, so pay attention. Little things can mean the most.

I would like to introduce you to each of my friends by name, share a few "family" photos, and experiences. There are four photos in this book that my husband took of me while I was praying, talking to heaven and to my friends. The cover photo of Archangel Chamuel was taken by my youngest daughter while we were on a hike in Sedona with Doreen Virtue. Doreen is the well-known author and founder of Angel Therapy. I personally photographed all of the other photos in this book. None of these pictures have been retouched. I have used many different cameras over the years, including a cell phone, pocket camera, as well as professional cameras, digital or film. It simply does not matter and makes no difference. They are always with me.

Anyone can take photos of their angels. They are always with you. Set your intention, fill your heart with love and gratitude, say your prayers, and ask them to appear. You may have to take quite a few pictures in the beginning as you find your rhythm. Don't give up. Practice, practice, practice. Keep snapping away with your camera.

Angels and Heaven's Divine Light Energy can appear as translucent or solid, as circles, orbs, flashes of light, tubes, sparklers, mists, or with angelic human like bodies and faces. Some are photographed in motion, while others float in midair. Welcome to my family photo album!

Chapter 2 God, Angels, & Orbs

1. Archangel Michael

Michael appears to me as a blue orb or mist. He is the head of the Archangels and the Angel of protection and justice. His name means "He who is like God" or "He who looks like God." Part of his job as a protector is to clear the earth of fear. Michael gives guidance and helps us have faith, courage, and strength. He is associated with the element of Fire and of the direction South. He is also the Angel of etheric cord cutting.

Etheric cords are energetic links from us to others. They can be good or they can be a drain. If you are angry with someone, thinking of them constantly, and sending daggers to them, this is a problem. You and the other person are caught up and bound to each other with harmful energy.

Ask Archangel Michael to "cut the etheric cords" of angry energy between you. Release the anger by

19

visualizing the cord-cutting freeing you from being tied to the other person. Visualize a beautiful blue light surrounding you. Mentally send rose-colored light and surround the other person with love and forgiveness. Surround yourself with a layer of rose pink light as well. Thank Michael and God for helping you to heal this situation. Amen, Ohm, and so it is.

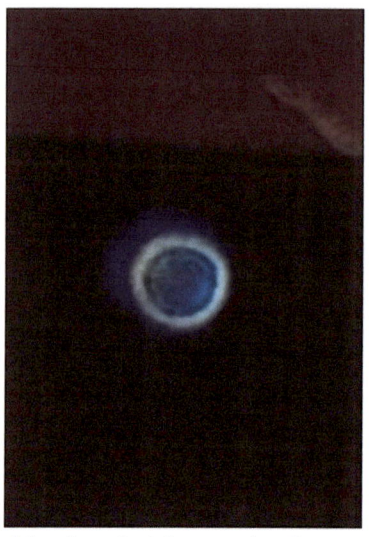

Archangel Michael provides protection and encourages us to make life changes that are required for your spiritual growth.

Spiritual growth happens to us in many different ways. We learn by our experiences.

My father-in-law was born in La Coruna, Spain, and so was his father. My father-in-law's mom died when he was a boy and his father remarried. The new stepmother was not kind to him. In response to the horrible environment, he mustered up his courage and found a job on a shipping freighter. At the age of fourteen he left his home country. Many months later the ship docked in Cuba. There he found a job as a logger. OMG! Does anyone today have a fourteen-year-old boy working full time in the woods logging trees? Unbelievable courage and survival instincts. (My husband is just like him.)

Later he found a job working for a family that had several daughters. After a few years, one would eventually become my mother-in-law. My sisters-in-law were born in Cuba. My husband

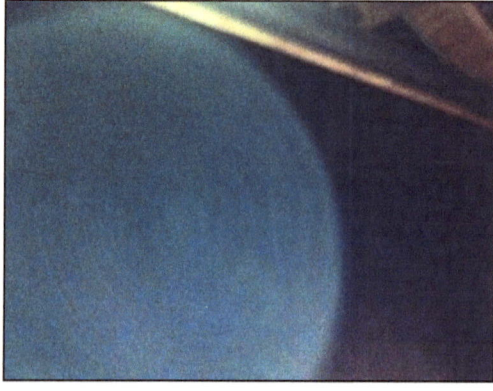

was conceived in Cuba and born in New York. My in-laws immigrated to the United States in 1944. The Cuban economy was a disaster and there were no jobs, so my in-laws agreed to come work in America for one year. Their plan was to earn money and then return to Cuba. Regrettably, during their absence the government of Cuba seized everything they owned. There was nothing left to go home to.

They shared an apartment in Manhattan with other family members, a very common practice at this time in the US. They worked their butts off and made a good life for themselves and their children.

After my father-in-law passed away, Yeya (my mother-in-law's nickname) eventually came to live with us. I found a bunch of her old pictures in a small shoebox in her closet. I sat down with her one day and we went through those pictures. There was a picture of my husband in a cowboy outfit on a pony while visiting Cuba. There was also a picture of my in-laws standing in front of a gate at their home in Cuba. She told me many stories and much about life in Cuba. She seemed homesick and missed my father-in-law terribly.

My husband and I talked and decided to ask my mother-in-law if she ever wanted to go back to Cuba. We would be happy to take her. She said she would love to go, but only after Castro was dead. She encouraged us to go without her. So we did.

We were amazed how an entire country could stand still in time, isolated, and cut off from the world. The Cuban people had nothing, yet they were happy and kind people.

We eventually found a driver to take us to the location where my in-laws used to live in Havana. It was quite a ride in an old 1950s vehicle with a wire coat hanger holding my door shut. The driver had to stop a few streets away because the road was too torn up to drive further. There were a few abandoned homes still standing on that road. We started walking over the rubble until we found their house. The iron and wood gate was still there, exactly like in the photo. We called to the driver to come see and asked him to take a picture of us. When we showed him the photo Yeya had given us, he was shocked. He said he couldn't believe the house was still standing and that we found it. My husband and I stood in the exact same spot in front of the gate, in the exact same position as they had so many years before, and our driver took the picture.

My mother-in-law was so blissful when we returned home and showed her our photo at their house in Cuba. I am sure Archangel Michael kept us safe, and at the same time, released the "etheric cord of pain" she had been carrying from Cuba for fifty years.

Chapter 2 God, Angels, & Orbs

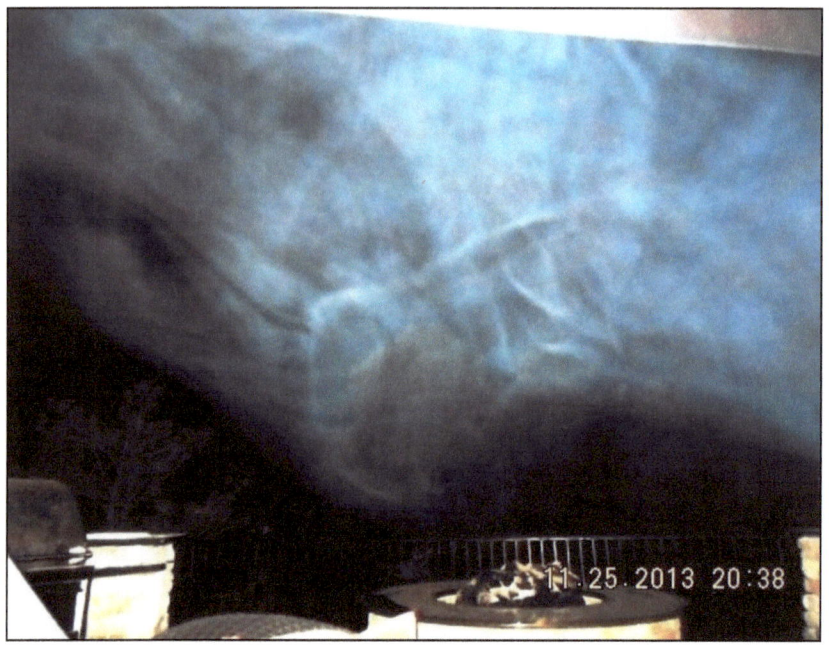

Archangel Michael on a cold clear night, no fire, around 8:30 pm.

Connect with Archangel Michael

Mind: Envision yourself surrounded by Archangel Michael's blue light. Close your eyes and feel a gentle cool mist surrounding your body.

Body: Dear Michael, please cut all etheric and energetic cords that unhealthily bind me to others. Please protect me from harm and encourage me as I proceed confidently on my life's path. Thank you. Amen.

Spirit: He will give his angels charge of you to guard you in all your ways. On their hands they will bear you up, lest you dash your foot against a stone.
-PSALMS 91:11-12

2. Archangel Gabriel

Gabriel always has a beautiful golden and white tone. Gabriel's name means "God is my strength." Gabriel is the Angel of child conception, helping with the process of adopting a child, birth, parenting, clear messages, revelations, and communication. Gabriel protects the Element of Water and the direction West. Gabriel is the Angel of resurrection, mercy, peace, purity, and harmony.

Archangel Gabriel brings me incredible clarity. When I pray for my children, ask for healing energy to raise my vibration, or to have God use me as a vessel of Love, Light, and Healing, my message is received and answered.

One time when we were traveling through South America, we visited Rio De Janiero in Brazil. Rio is a unique city, quite beautiful and sad at the same time. So many people have nothing and live in the favelas (slums). But the beach, Malecon, and mountains reflect the glitzy "lifestyles of the rich and famous" that we are accustomed to seeing on television. Such an incredible blend of opposites.

Before our ship docked, we had been talking to a gentleman on the cruise and became fast friends. He had grown up in Brazil, and his family had a jewelry store on the main drag. His name was Gabriel. (Serendipity?)

Gabriel said he was going to meet a friend who was a national hero for Brazil, a hang glider named "Mosquito." He asked us if we wanted to go hang-gliding with his friend. It took less than a second for me to open my mouth and scream YES! A phone call later.... Mosquito picked us up at the dock in his Land Rover. He drove like a crazy man, a million miles an hour through narrow streets, turns, and people, until we reached the top of a mountain overlooking the ocean. As we walked along a path through the trees, I could see a wooden platform which turned out to be the roof of a small shed. The roof was level to the ground, and the structure was lower and hung off the side of the cliff. This concerned me. What had I gotten us into?

Oh well, too late to suck my thumb and turn tail and run. I put on my big girl panties and told my husband that I would go first. If I died doing this stunt…well, he would still be alive and would be the more rational and logical parent to our kids. He is the voice of reason.

Mosquito and I harnessed up and ran as fast as we could off that wooden platform. I screamed as we fell, until the "wind beneath our wings" caught us and carried us up into the sky over the ocean. I am so grateful that I did not lay an egg or drop a potato into my underwear on takeoff.

Mosquito said that we would be flying for about twenty minutes before we would attempt our landing on Copacabana Beach. This sounded good to me -- a short flight, a sand landing. However, I did think about a hard landing face first into the ocean as another option.

Once we got to altitude Mosquito recognized a fellow hang-glider on the horizon. We flew over to him, and they chatted for a few minutes in Portuguese. Really? Wouldn't it be better to talk to his friend on the ground? The "sound" of this conversation intrigued me. We were very far apart, yet I could hear every word, as clear as a bell. It was dead silent and calm way up there in the sky. So peaceful, the strangest kind of silence I have ever experienced. The only noise I encountered was in my freaked-out head. When I gained my composure I settled into the ride and the experience: pure joy.

The entire world literally disappeared. The only thing I was aware of was my soul and the beautiful perspective of the ocean and Earth far below. I wondered to myself if this was what heaven felt like.

Mosquito asked me if I wanted to keep flying with him. I thought about my husband, and said a quick prayer to make sure he landed safely on the ground. Then I said yes! By changing the angle and distributed weight of our bodies, we were able to go higher and higher. When we reached peak altitude, several birds flew under our kite wing and "sailed" quietly with us. I was smiling so widely my cheeks hurt. We had been up there for about an hour and a half. Incredible, as it felt like ten minutes. Time stood still.

When Mosquito told me it was time for landing....thoughts of the egg and potato mixture came back into my mind. We traversed the beach, flew over skyscrapers, and decided where we were going to land. We dropped altitude fairly quickly, and he picked a lovely spot

on the beach, filled with umbrellas and a zillion people. Was he crazy? All I could envision was a bloody pile of body parts mixed with suntan oil and skewered with umbrella sticks. Something like chicken satay appetizers at a wedding.

We made our first fly-by, over the people's heads. I noticed that they started to pick up their belongings and their umbrellas and move out of the way. We made a second pass a little lower. It appeared that a runway was being made for us. On our final fly-by descent, before our "crash landing," I could see that we had a perfectly clear and lovely runway, with a crowd of thousands applauding us. We hadn't landed yet, so why were they cheering?

We floated down and glided gently above the beach until our feet were about three feet above the sand. Mosquito yelled for me to start running so I did. What a change from being weightless and feeling like I was in heaven, to hitting the earth and running in the hot heavy sand! Our landing was perfect, and Mosquito had two of his flight crew on the ground to catch the wings of the kite. No wonder people were cheering!

It wasn't until after we unharnessed that I looked back at the kite we had flown and saw that his name covered the entire underside on his kite. I then noticed that everyone had moved back to their place on the beach.

I guess if I were a soccer fan, and David Beckham needed to borrow my shower, I would make room for him, applaud him on his shower, support his arms so he wouldn't fall, dry him off, applaud him again, and send him on his way. It would be the right thing to do, wouldn't it? It would be my honor and privilege to help him.

My husband always tells me to "land the plane" (get to the point) when I share a long detailed story. So here is my landing.

I thought about how peaceful it must be in heaven, yet the feeling is not something many of us will experience while on Earth. NDE -- near death experiences happen -- to people here. They describe it as indescribable. I would describe heaven as being up in the sky, like I was, simultaneously getting a visit from Jesus and Archangel Gabriel, while understanding everything they said, in complete peaceful silence. I'll have to work with this scenario for now.

One never knows who you are going to meet and what will happen next. Don't they say to be kind to everyone, as you never know if you are entertaining an Angel? We were kind to a stranger named Gabriel, and look what happened.

Thank you to both of my Gabriel's....and for flying with a "mosquito."

Chapter 2 God, Angels, & Orbs

Connect with Archangel Gabriel

Mind: Imagine your body enveloped by a golden-white ball of light. Close your eyes and feel the warmth and goodness of the morning sun.

Body: Dear Gabriel, thank you for delivering divine messages on my behalf. Please clear away confusion and inspire me through my thoughts and dreams to fulfill my life's purpose. Thank you. Amen.

Spirit: Every blade of grass has its angel that bends over it and whispers, "Grow, grow."
- The Talmud

Chapter 2 God, Angels, & Orbs

3. Archangel Raphael

My Green Guy. Archangel Raphael is a healer in the Angelic realm. He helps with physical healing and guides us in matters involving our health. In Hebrew, Raphael means "God heals" or "He who heals." Many believe his name is derived from the Hebrew word Rophe, which means "medicine doctor." In Catholicism, Saint Raphael is the patron saint of healing, travelers, and matchmaking. Raphael is not shy about letting people know he is with them. Knowing that his presence is with you will help to comfort you and alleviate your stress along your way to a healthy recovery in whatever predicament you are experiencing.

When it comes to driving or traveling, he is my guy. If there is a traffic jam, he clears my way. When I ask for "snackbar parking", I usually get it. This special type of parking means you get the first and

best parking space by the Snackbar at a drive in movie! I also then do something nice for a stranger as my pay-it-forward. Opening a door, complimenting a stranger, or letting another driver go ahead of me balances things out. One good deed deserves another. Paying it forward feels really nice.

When it comes to health issues, Raphael is amazing. Imagine the color green. Think of the old Irish Spring soap commercials. Those commercials are filled with trees, mist, waterfalls, and beautiful green scenery. Imagine yourself there with a brilliant green sparking translucent light surrounding you. Ask Archangel Raphael to heal your entire body. Feel the gentle change in your cells as they are being repaired and restored.

The heart chakra color is green. Raphael glows as a green light. If you have a particular physical ailment that has manifested from "heartbreak," Raphael is your "go-to guy."

Every day when I am driving to the office I use this time for my conversation with heaven. I asked to be used as a vessel of love, light, and healing. I thank God, Jesus, Mary, Joseph, and all the Angels by name for helping me. I also ask my DPs (my dead people) and guides to be with me throughout the day. I ask for specific healing for the people I will see that day and I ask for specific healing for my family. I am not in charge of the master plan, but I still ask for precise things for others, if it is in their highest and best good. I then leave the rest of it up to the big guy, Amen.

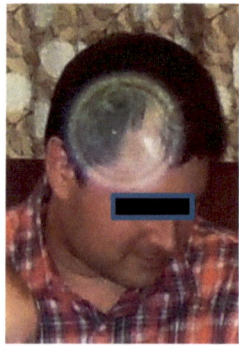

During my day at the office I am always surprised at what pops into my head about details I would have no logical or rational way of knowing.

For example: A mom brought in a grade school boy with digestive issues, skin rashes, and sleep problems. These issues had been going on for about a month, and their pediatrician was at a loss, as all of his tests were normal. The steroid cream and antibiotics were not working.

When I shook the young boy's hand, I could hear his grandfather's voice in my head. He also showed me and told me that his grandson had gotten a bearded dragon as a pet two months earlier. Obviously, the grandfather was crossed over, or he wouldn't be talking in my mind.

We all sat down at my desk, and I started to chat with the mom and her young son about what was going on. I then asked this young man if his bearded dragon had a hard time sleeping as well. I thought they were going to fall out of their chairs. There was no way I would know that detail about their lives, as I had just met them.

After their initial shock subsided, he told me that his dragon was afraid of the dark as well. He said he felt like someone was in his room. He was correct. It was his grandfather, who had passed away about two months prior. I gave him a polished heart-shaped prayer stone to place by his bed or hold in his hand when he went to bed and said his prayers. I told him he had nothing to be afraid of and that angels were always with him.

I asked him why he ate the bugs that he fed his dragon. This time neither mom nor son freaked out at this question. He simply told me that they were crunchy, and since his lizard liked them, so did he. We had just figured out why his belly was so upset, and why his lizard's food bill was so high.

I then asked him about his rashes. His grandfather showed me that he played too roughly and too much with this lizard. He was getting scratched by his buddy struggling to get away. He would also put this lizard in his bed with him at night, so they both would not be afraid. When morning came he would put Mr. Lizard back into his aquarium before his mom came into his room. This explained why his skin looked better before bed and was worse in the morning. Nightly sleepovers with a bearded dragon, who'd a thunk it?

A few homeopathic and naturopathic recommendations later, a change in his "snacking" (no more eating Mr. Lizard's bugs), a prayer stone for sleep, lizard sleeps in his own aquarium, boy sleeps in his bed without the lizard, and I felt we were on the right path.

The follow-up appointment five weeks later was really neat. The mom and her son couldn't have been happier. Her son's rash was completely gone. He was sleeping through the night restfully and was no longer afraid of the "person" in his room (his grandfather). His stomach no longer hurt, as he had stopped eating Mr. Lizard's dinner.

His mother told me that her son had been really close to her father. Grandpa's passing was sudden and very hard on the entire family, but especially difficult for her son. She told me that she could also sense her father was with her after his passing, but that she had never talked to her son about spiritual things, or where you go after you die, until after our first appointment.

She told me that with all of the grief they were experiencing after the funeral, they gave in and bought their son the bearded dragon he had always wanted. They thought it would help their son with his grief. That was when the wheels started to fall off their bus.

Without the help of Raphael and Grandpa, I might have found myself in the same predicament as his pediatrician. Looking beyond the some of the traditional causes of an ailment is not always easy. Stomachache, eczema, insomnia....eating bugs, lizard scratches, fear of the dark, and a spirit in your room....Mind, Body, Spirit.

I saw this young man and his mother many years later. He was now in high school. They didn't come in for anything specific, just a general overview and tune-up. He still had no rashes, no belly issues, and was sleeping great.

He still had the heart-shaped prayer stone I had given him. He was smiling ear to ear when he took it out of his pocket and showed it to me. They filled me in on the past seven or eight years and how everything had turned out great for him. Unfortunately, Mr. Lizard had passed away. I am sure his grandfather now has a pet lizard in heaven.

Health issues and healing present in many different ways. The underlying catalyst can be a surprise, as well as the path to fix it.

When this young boy's grandfather passed away suddenly, it caused a change in the family dynamics. When we address all areas

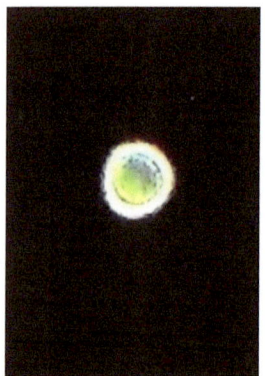

of our life and are open to every possibility, our Mind, Body, and

Spirit come back into balance. Funny how Spirit energy can change our lives.

I am always grateful to have Archangel Raphael at my side, and I will always smile when I think of green bearded dragons.

Connect with Archangel Raphael

Mind: In your mind's eye, picture the injured cells in your body being cleansed and restored with a sparkly brilliant green light.

Body: Dear Raphael, thank you for assisting me in healing my mind, body, and soul. Please protect me during my daily travels and help me to comfort others who are hurting and in need of healing in their lives. Thank you. Amen.

Spirit: I saw them with my bodily eyes as clearly as I see you. And when they departed, I used to weep and wish they would take me with them.
-Joan of Arc 1412 - 1431

4. Archangel Uriel

I see Uriel as a white light with a golden touch, a spiral orb, and as a flash. Uriel's name means "God is light," "Gods light," or "Fire of God," because he illuminates situations and gives prophetic information or warnings. Uriel is known as the angel of wisdom. He shines light into the darkness of confusion. People ask for Uriel's help in seeking God's will before making decisions, or to come up with creative ideas or learn new information. Uriel also helps us to solve problems, resolve conflicts,

and let go of anxiety or anger that can block us from recognizing true wisdom or guidance. In art, Uriel is often depicted carrying either a book or a scroll, which symbolizes wisdom.

Another representation connected with Uriel is an open hand holding a flame, which symbolizes God's truth. Uriel defends the elements of Earth and of the East. Uriel is the Angel of nature, visions, prophecy, clear thinking, intellectual understanding, calm energy, and epiphanies. When I am deep in thought about a particular situation or intensely reading a book, a bright light, flash, or spiraling orb shows up to help me.

When I am concerned or worried, I will also see a flash, somewhat like a pinpoint burst of light. When I am really playful, like a child, Uriel also spirals for me.

I see and feel a curved tube of light energy when I specifically ask for knowledge, enlightenment, or a solution to a complex issue. Before I know it, an idea or solution pops into my head.

We were on a boat heading down the Rhine River in Germany. I was thinking about my German language teacher in junior high school. Her name was Judy, and she eventually married the football coach, Tom. I had painted a picture of Tom's dog for him, back in the day when dinosaurs roamed the Earth (when I was younger). I thought about how kind she was to me and how she had made it possible and paid for me to go to a German language camp one summer. That camp was in the forest and on a river. The Rhine River now reminded me of that river and how lucky I was to be experiencing those same happy feelings many years later.

I also thought about how much she had taught me about the history of Germany (pre-psychotic Hitler era) and the richness of its

culture. I loved her very much. She never judged my lack of family or nice things, like the other students had. She always welcomed my constant barrage of questions and would bring me her books from home to read about Germany.

(We only had one schoolbook in class to learn the language and the history.) I said a prayer for her, thanking her for her influence in my young life. She was killed in a drunken driving accident shortly after she married the coach.

As we floated down the Rhine we came upon one of the over five hundred plus medieval castles in Germany. This one was named Rheinfels Castle. It was over eight hundred years old. It had been occupied by many families. In order to acquire a castle, you could build your own over hundreds of years, or you had to "eliminate" the prior owners. What a way to negotiate a real estate deal: Give it to me, or I will chop off your head!

The incredible castle was situated on a hilltop, and I wondered just how long and how hard it would be to build such a home during those eight hundred years. The castle was always being added on to and repaired after hostile takeover attempts.

It was raining pretty hard once we climbed up to the entrance. There were very few visitors that day because of the mud and the rain -- so to me it was perfect. We walked around, climbed over rubble, and learned much about the castle and its history. I asked the curator what was down a blocked-off set of stairs. He told me that they had accidently collapsed a wall under the castle while doing repair work. Behind that collapsed wall was a homeopathic Apothecary, hundreds of years old. It had been sealed up to protect it during one of the many battles.

I begged him to let me see it. I told him what I did for a living and everything else I could think of….and then I begged some more. He finally laughed and said sure. Down those stairs I ran, with him and my husband close behind me.

He told me nothing had been touched or moved in hundreds of years, so to please be careful. They had not yet started to catalogue or record their find.

I started to tell him what was in each cobalt or amber glass vial or bottle, and what they were used for. He was quite surprised and pleased as he wrote down everything I said. It was so much fun! There were signs posted outside of the Apothecary excavation for the workers and future visitors that said "No pictures, No flash, Do Not Touch." I begged him to let me take a picture in the Apothecary. Please, please, please, just one picture. He looked at me as if I had those two heads again, but smiled and said yes. I squealed like a pig! My husband took the picture. When I looked at it more closely, I could see my angel orb friends were scattered about, enjoying the Apothecary as well.

When we finally got a break in the down pouring rain, we made a run for it back to the boat. I settled into my plastic lawn chair in the front of the boat as my brain went into high gear again and matched the smile on my face. My poor poor wonderful husband had survived yet another crazy adventure.

I thought about a book I had read as a child, *Willy Wonka and the Chocolate Factory*. I was also the kid who read every book my German teacher, Judy, had shared with me about Germany, its culture, weird facts, and surprisingly, about medical treatment and torture from hundreds of years before. Here I was as an adult now, and feeling like Charlie must have felt when he went into the Chocolate Factory. I was as happy as a kid in a candy store.

I thank Archangel Uriel for helping me to read and comprehend about twenty to thirty books per year. I thank Uriel as well for helping me to read extremely fast and to be able to store all of that information for easy recall when needed. "Knowledge" gives us the power to change things for the better.

"Understanding/comprehension" gives us the ability to see all sides of an issue and avoid disaster. My willingness to share my knowledge helped the curator find out what was in his Apothecary. His understanding of my childlike exuberant behavior concerning his castle and long-lost find, made me feel like Charlie in the Chocolate Factory. A win-win for both of us -- nice job Uriel.

Connect with Archangel Uriel

Mind: Think of a situation or a problem that needs a touch of wisdom to resolve. See your answer coming to your mind as a spiraling flash of light.

Body: Dear Uriel, please shed light on this situation, bring me clarity, and help me to release the tension I hold in my body. Thank you. Amen.

Spirit: An angel can illumine the thought and mind of man by strengthening the power of vision and by bringing within his reach some truth which the angel himself contemplates.
- St. Thomas Aquinas

5. Archangel Chamuel

Archangel Chamuel is a beautiful, vibrant rose pink color. Archangel Chamuel's name means "He who sees God" or "'He who seeks God". In Hebrew the translation of the name Chamuel also means "comfort" and "compassion." Chamuel is a dynamic leader in the angelic hierarchy and is known to protect the world and us from fearful or lower energies. Ask Chamuel to help you find comfort, unconditional love, tolerance, gratitude, protection, and to intervene on your behalf in situations requiring universal or your own personal peace.

These photos were taken by my youngest daughter while we were on a hike in Sedona, Arizona, with Doreen Virtue. My daughter took about twenty pictures by herself, and every photo has Chamuel doing something different each time.

Earlier that day we were having a conversation about how horrible things could happen to good people. I told her that maybe the lessons in some horrific events were to lead us to realize how much we are actually loved.

Archangel Chamuel brings unconditional love and helps our souls to heal after unspeakable tragedy, illness, or injury.

When I was in college I was offered a work program to pay for my meals. I happily said yes, as I was as poor as a church mouse. I was assigned to work two hours a day in the Chancellor's office. His name was Dr. Lofy. After a few weeks I settled in and became friends with him. He shared much about his life and would sit at the front desk with me during his lunchtime. He told me he wanted to do something nice for his wife for their anniversary. I decided I would do something nice for him. I painted him a picture of two zebras prancing, just like he had described to me about their trip to South Africa. He was thrilled. A few days later he brought me a photo they had taken of two zebras. To my shock, the photo was exactly as I had painted them.

He asked me how I was doing financially, what I was doing with the "lunch money" job, and why I wasn't eating at the cafeteria. Simple answer: it cost less to eat animal crackers and soup then it did to pay for the cafeteria plan, and I was using the extra money to pay for my books. He offered me another job, babysitting his two children once a week. I said yes.

The first time I went to their beautiful ivy-covered stone home, I gaped in awe. It looked and felt like something from a fairytale book, with a beautiful arched wooden front door. When I rang the bell, his wife answered and invited me in. Their children were not at home, so I was a little confused.

They had a petite tri-colored sheltie named Portnoy. What a sweet sweet dog. He was named after the book *Portnoy's Complaint*. I sat at the table as Dr. Lofy's lovely wife, Mary, told me about their family and children. Dr. Lofy walked in and joined us. We chatted a bit more and then started the tour of their home. When we got to the study, its walls packed with books, he asked me to sit in his "meditation" chair. I complied. He grabbed a headset and told me they wanted me to listen to their favorite music, because I would be playing it for their children before bed. His wife turned on the reel-to-reel tape machine. He told me it was an actual recording from Rome, performed for the Pope and Dr. Lofy, in private. He then told me he used to be a Cardinal in Rome. I listened, stunned. I had never heard such heavenly music or voices.

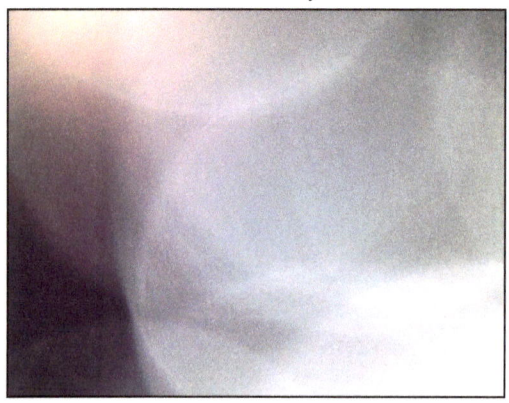

When the music session was complete, The Lofy's told me about how they met. She was a nun, he was a Cardinal, they fell in love and were excommunicated. They were two of the most kind and compassionate souls I have ever met. The church lost two angels in my opinion.

I babysat their children for a semester, once a week, and loved every minute of it. The first time they paid me, I corrected them on their math. I was to make five dollars an hour for two children. Fifteen dollars for three hours. She gave me forty dollars, and I felt badly for her mistake. I put all of the money back into her hand. He took the money out of her hand and put it back into my hand, and said there was no mistake on their part. He told me how much he enjoyed my being in his office, that he and his family really cared for me, and that at the end of the semester everything would change. They both thanked me for the painting of the zebras. These were not people, these were angels. These people showed me unconditional love, and we weren't even biologically related. Family is who loves you, not just who gives birth to you.

Many years later my husband and I were in South Africa, north of Johannesburg and south of Mozambique. We stopped when we came across a herd of about three hundred zebras. I thought it would be a good idea to jump out of the Land Rover and talk to the zebras, up close, though I shared these thoughts with no one but myself.

I had an apple in my hand before we came upon them. When I saw these "Fruit Striped Gum Ponies," BAZINGA, I decided I would share my apple with them, just like I wanted to do with them when I was a kid. I bit my apple into many pieces and piled the pieces into my free hand. I jumped out of the Land Rover very quietly, so as not to frighten my new friends. Everyone else was unloading and doing whatever they were doing. I was very gently walking while talking to my new friends. I did not realize that at the time I was actually wearing a black and white striped shirt, black capris, and a black baseball cap. I looked sort of like a zebra without a tail. I continued talking to them, asking them if they wanted an apple.

That was rather weird. How would they know if they wanted an apple grown in Europe? Silly me. However, apparently they had read some books about apples. Four of them walked closer. Then three of them met me in the middle. The rest of the herd didn't move. Reminded me of the movie *Brave Heart*...before the massacre. To my delight, the three zebras stopped walking toward me, to let me walk right up to them. Still talking, I held my hand out with the apple pieces. Their noses went wacko and their heads bobbed. I held my hand low, since they are short, four-legged souls, to let them sniff and take the apple pieces into their mouths. They were quite polite and took turns. The apple was gone in less than a minute. Now what was I supposed to do?

I heard our friend, our African guide, and my husband yelling to me. They sounded really freaked out. I looked back toward them, only to see a Swiss, a South African, and a Cuban man with horror slapped across their faces. I turned back to my striped friends and told them to have a really good day and thanks for the chat. I told them they were good zebras, and scratched their chins a little.

Instead of turning tail to run, I walked backwards, while still telling them what good zebras they were. They just stood there watching me, all of them. I was aware that things could go horribly wrong and my head could be kicked in like a soggy melon. But I knew in my soul that was not their plan for me that day. I honestly could feel in my gut that I was supposed to "break bread" with my new found friends.

Everything turned out nicely as I reached the Land Rover and all three men recovered from their panic about my welfare and my crazy decision. Those lovely zebras got a snack they had probably never tasted in their lives...and I got an amazing soul grin. As I climbed back into our vehicle I thought about the painting I had done of the zebras in college. I thought about the photo they shared with me *after* I had given them the painting. All I could do was smile, as they were correct -- zebras are really happy, kind souls...and I had just experienced unconditional love and protection, up close and personal.

So how do these two events relate to each other and to Archangel Chamuel? Well, as a reminder, Archangel Chamuel helps us find comfort, unconditional love, tolerance, gratitude, protection, and intervenes on our behalf to help bring about situations that bring us peace. I have always loved horses and zebras. I felt called to paint those zebras in college. The Lofy's showed me unconditional love and acceptance. I dressed like a zebra that day in Africa. We came across that herd completely by accident -- or was it? I felt called to share my apple with them. They reciprocated by giving me the gift of their company, the pure joy of the experience, and by not trampling me into a bucket of bloody oatmeal.

I have noticed many times in life that when we feel all alone, we really are not. If we are open and lead with pure intention, Archangel Chamuel protects us, reminds us, and helps us to find and feel unconditional love. Works every time, regardless of whether we have two legs or four.

That said, I do not recommend walking up to a herd of wild zebras to share your snack. It could turn out to be more like riding a skateboard off a cliff.

My appreciation to Archangel Chamuel, and thanks for keeping my crazy butt safe, and loved.

Connect with Archangel Chamuel

Mind: Picture yourself at sunrise standing in a field of pink wild roses. Breathe in the aroma of the flowers and the dew. Close your eyes.

Body: Dear Chamuel, please surround me with heaven's unconditional love. Please assist me in maintaining gratitude and hope while I am going through this difficult time. Thank you. Amen.

Spirit: Angels descending, bring from above echoes of mercy, whispers of love.
-Fanny Crosby 1820-1915

6. Archangel Metatron

My ruby red moon. In many of my paintings I have included a red orb or circle. It wasn't until many years later that I figured out why the painting wasn't complete until I added Archangel Metatron. I see him as a ruby red/orange orb.

Metatron is known as the Angel of life. He guards the Tree of Life and records the good deeds people do on Earth, as well as what happens in heaven, into the Book of Life (which is also known as the Akashic record). People sometimes ask for Metatron's help to discover their personal spiritual gift and to learn how to use it to bring glory to God and make the world a better place. Metatron is an energetic angel who has a special place in his heart for children, especially those who are spiritually gifted, and pets. He offers his service, wisdom, sacred geometry, and esoteric healing.

Sacred geometry is a curious thing. Sacred geometry is used in the design and building of churches, temples, mosques, altars, holy wells, religious art, and more.

Sacred geometry has its roots in nature and mathematical principles. Even the honeybee constructs hexagonal cells to hold its honey.

Pythagoras is credited for identifying harmonic ratios in music. He believed that sound frequency could "harmonize" an "out of tune body." Leonardo da Vinci's drawings of the geometric principle of the human body are also astonishing. I believe Metatron guided them both.

Archangel Metatron helps me to find balance in my paintings and logic in my practice. He listens, shows up, and helps me find the good in challenging situations.

A few years ago I had an especially tough day at my practice. I had seen three separate teenagers that day, all of whom had made an attempt at suicide and failed. A common theme they all shared was that they felt they were different spiritually than other teens their age. They felt they didn't fit in, were "freaks", and were in emotional pain all of the time. They wanted to end their life because they were tired of this world. Was this Mind, Body, or Spirit? It was all three. Sadly, they all had a genetic

predisposition for depression or anxiety. They all had poor nutrition and terrible diets. They all felt everyone else's pain and carried it with them. That is called Clairsentience. Each one of their stories took me back to parts of my childhood.

When I arrived home that night I shared my feelings with my husband. I decided I needed to listen to some music outside and meditate. I asked Archangel Metatron to show up and help me. I felt a warm tingle, saw him in my mind, and decided to take his picture. He obliged and followed me around the deck, getting brighter and brighter. I love it and appreciate it when I ask for a sign or proof that my thoughts are heard, and they deliver. I went to bed that night with hope and a new insight on how to help unique souls balance and thrive in a chaotic world. I am very happy to report that all three of those tormented teens are alive and thriving today.

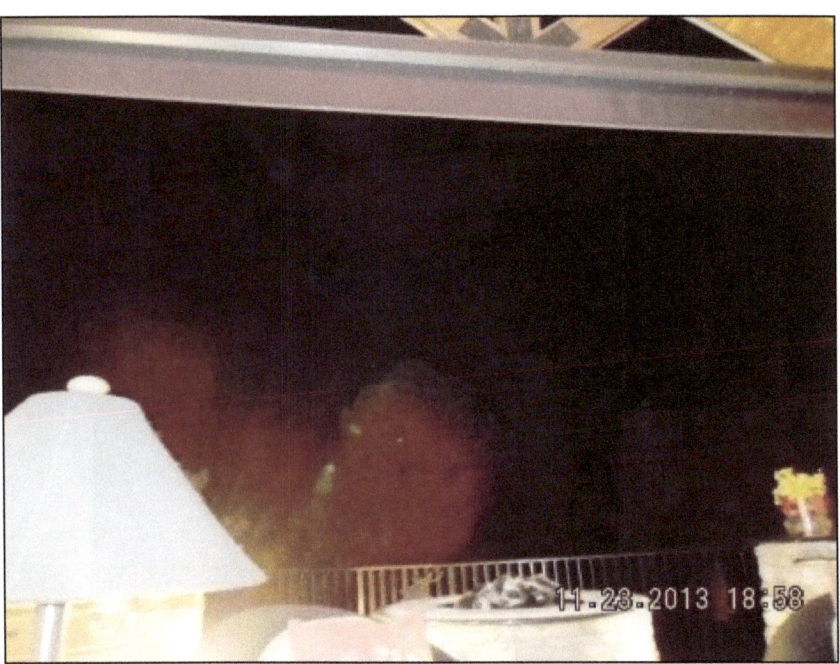

My husband and Portnoy (named after the Lofy's dog). You can see three beautiful orbs staying close to them both. Portnoy passed away a few days later.

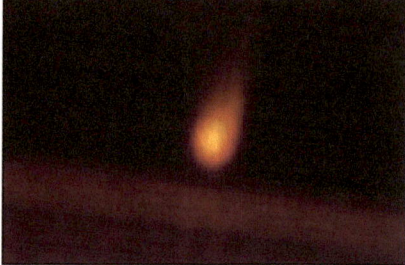

Archangel Metatron loves animals and animals have always brought me great joy. Just because they may be wild, or unpopular breeds or species, does not mean that they don't feel or have a soul. I believe they are here to help us and we are here to help them. They give us one hundred times more love and respect than most people give to each other. Helping animals is a good way to get grounded and give thanks for our abundance and abilities. Animals have distinct personalities and traits. Have you ever noticed that people have pets that resemble themselves? Animals have angels and guides. Many of you will find angels and orbs in photos of your pets if you just take a second look. For example, in this photo of Hunter, our larger white dog, you can see Archangel Metatron is just above his tail, bright red/orange orb with a flame like point.

Chanel is our little white dog, here seen lying on the bed. You can see five guardian-angel orbs above her head in one photo and two in the other photo.

Animals have souls and help us in our journey. If they pass over before us, they will be there to greet us when we arrive. It feels good to soothe an animal, doesn't it? Have you ever held your pet or a stray and never wanted to put them down? As if they were reading your mind and you were reading theirs? Unspoken words of love and communication happen all the time in this world. If you have not seen the true story of a dog and

his man that was made into the movie *Hachi*, you simply must. This movie will truly change the way you perceive nonverbal communication. Animals do not express themselves with human words; they express themselves with feelings, expressions, intention, and thoughts. Communicating telepathically with animals is pretty easy for most people. If you have a pet you probably do it every day.

How do your pets know what you are thinking? Why do you

talk to them if they don't have a soul? Do you talk to your coffee cup and ask it if it missed you while you were gone? Probably not. When our souls connect with another soul we are forever linked. When souls pass over we talk to them in our minds. We just "know" they hear us. We are not surprised when we ask our angels or deceased loved ones to show us a sign, and then they do. We feel grateful and calmed by the sign and their presence. Feeling, sensing, and communicating with God, Spirit, Source, or Angels feels just as pleasant; it is not a scary thing. Have you ever heard your dog bark at imaginary flying objects in your house? When animals do this, they are usually watching Angels play. This is a great time to ask Archangel Metatron to watch over and protect our beloved little buddies.

I have some good ideas on how to help your animal friends. To learn more about each tip, you can just type into your computers search bar some of the topic information from the section below. You will find a tremendous amount of information and resources.

Consider acupressure or the use of a Red LED laser light (660nm) for anxiety or stress. Acupressure points can be used to calm their spirit by releasing anxiety, stress, and worry while also addressing behavioral concerns or hyperactivity. Some of my favorite points for acupressure are; Conception Vessel 14 (CV14) Anxiety, Governing Vessel 20 (GV 20) Anxiety, Heart 7 (HT 7) Anxiety, and Spleen 1 (SP 1) Grounding.

You can use pheromone spray or collars for cats and dogs. Separation from the pack can be very difficult for some pets. We send our children off to camp with special blankets, pictures, or stuffed animals to help with their separation anxiety. Our children know they are coming home at the end of the week. Puppies and kittens "know" they are not being returned home to their mother. Call it instinct. If we have a pet we should think about their emotional wellbeing. No one wants to feel abandoned. DAP or similar products work wonderfully.

Brain tones and special music can be played to help your pets. Check out iTunes or a music store for calming music for animals.

If they don't sleep with you, give them something that smells like you to sleep with, like an old, unwashed t-shirt.

Joy and play. No one likes to be bored out of their mind. Make sure your pets have room to move and play toys. Consider adding an indoor fence to your kennel.

Clean water, excellent quality food, and vitamins. Cows eat grain and grass; canines and felines eat meat. Don't feed your pet the wrong type of food, regardless of advertising. I have never seen a dog run into a field to steal and hoard his own supply of soybeans. If your pet has a medical condition, educate yourself and get her proper medical care. If your pet does not have a medical condition, educate yourself on how to keep her that way.

Try thinking your words to your pets. Talk to them in your mind. Set your intention to have them respond. A great time to try this technique is when your pet is lying on the floor, not facing you, but just hanging out. Think in your mind "Chanel's a good dog." Use your pets name: "Dilbert's a good ferret." Think it with enthusiasm several times, many times, over and over in your head. Then just sit back watch his tail start to wag as he gets up from lying at your feet and jumps into your lap. I have done this many times over the years. Each time I just smile. It works. Have fun with this. This is a great way to practice the power of intention. Whatever we send out over our "radio waves" will eventually be picked up by someone.

A big thank you to Archangel Metatron for watching over our spiritually gifted children, and our fury, smooth, or feathered friends.

Connect with Archangel Metatron

Mind: Close your eyes, imagine that you are sitting on an iron bench by the ocean. You are observing a beautiful red sunset as it paints the sky.

Body: Dear Metatron, please help me to recognize and develop my God given talents. Please help me to be kind and supportive as I share these gifts for the benefit of others. Thank you. Amen.

Spirit: We are like children, who stand in need of masters to enlighten us and direct us; God has provided for this, by appointing his angels to be our teachers and guides.
-St. Thomas Aquinas

7. Archangel Sandalphon

Sandalphon is the conductor of my vibrational orchestra. When I play music while meditating or praying, he coordinates the other angels into a delightful symphony of movement. As I change the song they change their direction. I usually play Snatam Kaur's music: "Take Me In," "By Thy Grace," "Servant of Peace," "Guru Guru Wahe Guru," and "Teree Meher Da Bolanaa," or something similar.

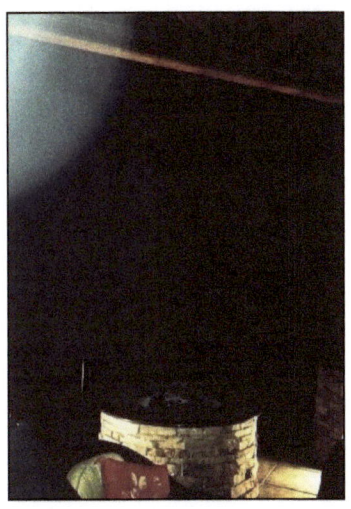

His color is a light cool turquoise green. He is generally described as extremely tall. Sandalphon's name is derived from the word for "brother" in Greek, a reference to his twin brother, the Archangel Metatron. Sandalphon's job is to receive and deliver human prayers to God. Sandalphon is also the Angel of music and sound healing. Music soothes the savage beast, and me.

Archangel Sandalphon has been with me since I was about ten or eleven year old, this time period was during the 1970s. Just to give you an idea on what the social scene was like then, here are a few fun facts.

President Nixon resigned. Eighteen-year-olds were finally allowed to vote. Eleven Israeli athletes were killed by terrorists at the Olympic Games in Munich, Germany. We gave the Panama Canal back to Panama. The Three Mile Island nuclear plant had a partial meltdown. The Bee Gees, Barry Manilow, the Doobie Brothers, and John Denver were at the top of the music charts. And of course, *Charlie's Angels* came on T.V.

Music was my diversion in life during this time period. Every song I heard seemed to have meaning for

Chapter 2 God, Angels, & Orbs

me. One song lyric in particular hit me hard. "Take me home, country roads," sung by John Denver. When I heard it I would get an overwhelming feeling of sadness and loneliness. I would think about the day I prayed for God to "take me home" as a child. I would also think about the light that filled the room and the message that all would be okay. What started as a sad song for me turned into one that brings me joy and reminds me that there is so much more.

A goofy thing happened to me during my freshman year in college. I was in an anatomy class that was populated by boys, and me. I never spoke in class or talked to anyone. One day all of the guys had on Doobie Brothers t-shirts. For some unknown reason I opened my mouth. I asked them why they all had the same shirts on. They were quite surprised that I actually spoke to them. They told me they were going to the concert that night. I decided to say more. I said, "Isn't it cool that they are all brothers, they don't look alike, they all have great

voices, and they have such a weird last name?"

Once again I felt like I had two heads sticking out of my neck. They laughed at me and said that the Doobie Brothers were not real brothers, that their last names were not Doobie, and that they called themselves that because they smoked reefer together. "Reefer?" Oh, I finally got it -- pot, reefer, joint, doobie. Mortified at my stupidity, I felt my face burning. I did not speak again during that class. I must have lived under a large rock in the forest as well as being a lone wolf. Back to my music, including the Doobie Brothers.

Something many people do not know much about is Vibroacoustic Therapy. It is a very gentle, noninvasive, and profound modality for healing. Music is sound and vibration. Our cells resonate with countless frequencies that can be matched with musical sound vibration. Vibroacoustic therapy is based on the principle that life is vibration. Matter, including our bodies, vibrates constantly on a multitude of frequencies. Sound and music also vary in vibrational frequency. When these frequencies of sound and/or music are converted to vibration and introduced to our body, they can be utilized to bring the body into a state of healthy resonance.

If you have ever sat next to someone playing a cello or a violin, for example, you can "feel" the musical vibrations deep in your soul. A more extreme example would be to stand in front of a speaker at a rock concert. You get the picture!

Our bodies are composed largely of water – about 70% for an adult and about 90% for a newborn. This water is set into motion when our body is exposed to these sound vibrations. As the water is moved by the vibration, our molecules will react and communicate with each other. As this communication ensues, harmony and a healthy resonance is restored in our bodies.

The pioneer of Vibroacoustic Therapy, Olav Skille, a Norwegian scientist, presented VAT to the world in the 1960s. Since then, this treatment modality has grown and blossomed with the advent of computers and advances in science. VAT has been used as a tool to help patients with different health conditions including: fibromyalgia, chronic pain syndrome, PTSD, multiple sclerosis, Parkinson's, insomnia, depression, anxiety, arthritis, ADD, ADHD, asthma, addiction, COPD, bed sores, Rett Syndrome, and more.

Search the internet for "Vibroacoustic Therapy." You will find many research articles and practical applications for this modality. Music truly is medicine.

Archangel Sandalphon really rocks, actually, he *vibrates*!

Connecting with Archangel Sandalphon

Mind: Take a deep breath, exhale, relax your eyes. You are floating in a pool of crystal-clear turquoise water. You can hear and *feel* Heavens beautiful music as the sound vibrations permeate the water and your body.

Body: Dear Sandalphon, please deliver my prayers to God as you soothe and heal my body with divine musical vibrations from Heaven. Thank you. Amen.

Spirit: Music is well said to be the speech of angels, in fact, nothing among the utterances allowed to man is felt to be so divine. It brings us near to the infinite.
-Thomas Carlyle 1795 - 1881

8. Archangel Ariel

Archangel Ariel shows up in my pets' pictures as an orb with a faint shade of white with pink and yellow hues, especially when they are resting or just calmly hanging out. Ariel's name means "Lion or lioness of God." Ariel helps with healing and protecting nature, which includes the animals, fish, and birds, especially the wild ones. Ariel also oversees the elemental kingdom, Earth, fairies, bodies of water, the state of the environment, and connecting to nature.

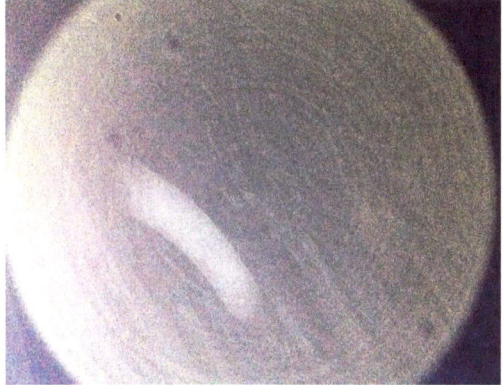

I have always felt a kinship with animals. Here I am in my winter coat with my pet mink, Eleanor, poking out from my winter coat collar. I have always had pets, including but not limited

Chapter 2 God, Angels, & Orbs

to ferrets, cows, a steer named Harry, a horse named Snowball, dogs, cats, fish, a salamander, a rabbit, various wild animals, and a coyote that I named Mary, with her pups.

Archangel Ariel is also associated with the wind. I will hear what sounds like a faint wind chime in my ear or feel a slight breeze and goosebumps when I sense her presence.

The next time you decide to take a walk in the park, go to the beach, or hang out in your back yard, ask Archangel Ariel to join you. If you find even the smallest piece of trash, pick it up and dispose of it properly. Say a blessing for the wonderful Earth that we live on. Don't be surprised if something unusually nice happens to you that day because of your good deed. Ah, serendipity.

Well, I know a wonderful human soul named Ariel as well. Her full name is Ariel Hardy, the Energy Healer. Google her, as she is an amazing energy healer, self-taught. She is the most incredible being I have met who is a mix between Earth elemental, human, and angel. Fragile, strong, talented, gifted...like when someone gives you a spun sugar ornament at the holidays. That is the way I would describe her.

Hope you like this, Ariel!

Some of the most fragile things in life can be the most important. We commonly dismiss the plant in a large field that is not thriving. We frequently dismiss the underdog. Those who take a risk on the underdog, and believe they can do it, tend to find themselves with a wonderful soul-based payoff. Those who simply bet on the underdog for expansive gain without pure intention generally do not win with those odds. Thus we have Las Vegas. Just think of every movie out there for us to see. There is a movie, *Rudy*, which is a true story about overcoming obstacles, bravery, and determination. We cheer when Rudy, the Notre Dame Football player, succeeds. I love that movie. But how many of us would have supported a "Rudy" during his trials and difficulties? Well, one person did, and then a few more followed. We all cheer when we hear incredible stories of survival and the people who helped those more fragile. When we act with an open heart and a giving hand, Archangel Ariel will help us overcome obstacles and achieve our goals in life. What a cool angel.

I adore Archangel Ariel.

Chapter 2 God, Angels, & Orbs

    In July of 2015 we were fishing on the Sea of Cortez. I was talking to heaven in my mind, asking Ariel to bring us some fish, and thanking God for such a beautiful day. I asked for a sign that I was heard. I then saw an enormous whale shark off in the distance. A whale shark is actually the world's largest fish. They are about 65 feet long and 75,000 pounds. We immediately cut the engines to our boat and waited to see what she would do. She suddenly disappeared back into the sea. A few moments later I saw a strange movement and diamond like sparkles in the water behind our boat; she had a baby and it was headed towards us. I squealed so loud that her baby stopped, flipped around, and started to swim away. I apologized to the little one and asked her to come back. Everyone on the boat thought I was crazy for talking to a fish. Guess what? She turned back around as I spoke to her, telling her how pretty she was. I asked her if I could touch her and take her picture. She swam right up to me. As I hung over the boat to pet her head, she rose up to meet my hand. I thanked her profusely for her generosity and kind spirit. I asked her to wait so I could take her picture, she happily obliged before she swam away. Isn't she lovely? Sometimes, all we have to do is ask. Thank you Ariel.

Archangel Ariel outside.   Ariel, me, and Archangel Ariel inside.

Connecting with Archangel Ariel

Mind: Partially close your eyes. Perceive a lush green forest and feel the grassy ground beneath your feet. Notice the butterfly's in the air, bunny's eating grass, and the fawn with its mother in the distance. Relax your body.

Body: Dear Ariel, please bless and protect Mother Earth and all of its precious creatures. Bring me an opportunity to help make our Earth a better place to live for all. Guide me to have a open heart and a giving hand. Thank you. Amen.

Spirit: "If all the beasts were gone, men would die from a great loneliness of spirit, for whatever happens to the beasts also happens to the man. All things are connected."
-Chief Seattle of the Suwamish Tribe, letter to President Franklin Pierce

9. Archangel Jophiel

Archangel Jophiel lights up for me as a blend of soft misty white, yellow, and pink tones. Jophiel's name means "Beauty of God." Jophiel helps us to imagine beautiful and gorgeous things to help us create, manifest, and attract more splendor into our lives. Illumination, wisdom, and perception. Thoughts of beauty and love. Jophiel is the Angel of artists and an inspiration to me. In this photo you will notice that the fire pit is not on, my house is not burning down, and it is a clear, calm beautiful evening.

During high school I needed money for a letter jacket. I painted an oil on canvas of the beloved German shepherd owned by the football coach. He paid me fifty dollars for this painting, which put me halfway to my goal. My first commissioned painting, yeah! I have continued to paint angels, horses, various animals, and abstract art using multiple mediums.

My inspiration comes to me in my dreams. I go to sleep and wake up with a painting completed in my head. I can see every layer. I see it in three dimensions. I see the finished painting. I scratch it out with a pencil on paper so I can get on with my day. It drives me nuts. I can't get it out of my head until I finish the painting. Once it is done the stress goes away, and I honestly feel relief for a job well done. I can spend the next ten or twenty years looking at the various paintings and not want to change a thing. I have always wished I'd had an art class or two. But I decided I didn't want to ruin a worthy thing, so no art classes. I am self-taught and heavenly guided; that is good enough for me.

About eighteen years ago my husband said we needed to have people over for a dinner party. He said I needed to socialize more. As usual this triggered my childhood fear and social anxiety. Although in a state of terror, I complied. I went to work creating the most amazing dinner for twelve that anyone could ever eat. I made sure the table was perfect, the house was perfect, and that the guests would have a perfect time. I kept myself uber-busy in the kitchen during dinner so I wouldn't have to talk to anyone. My plan was working perfectly too, until one guest, a gentleman I did not know, started asking questions. He was wandering around our house, looking at all of my paintings. I had twenty-one paintings hung on the walls at that time. He asked my husband where we had gotten the art and who the artist was. I was about to die. My husband told him that I had painted every one of them. By the end of the evening I had been cornered by him and I agreed to an artist's opening at a gallery.

My opening was held with another artist. I thought that would be great so the attention would be off of me. Big surprise -- I was paired with the dealer's Rembrandt etchings. Rembrandt wasn't physically present to entertain or talk to anyone that night. I honestly thought people would just look at my paintings, not buy them. I was not worried that I would lose any of my babies.

I was wrong. Many of my paintings sold that night. People would come up to me and ask me what "trauma" was my inspiration for various paintings. Really? I did not cut off an ear or feel that any trauma had brought them to fruition. My paintings bring me joy, peace, a connection to my angelic friends and God. I simply told them that I see them in my mind. Most people wanted a much better story from me. When a painting was marked sold, other people came up to me and asked me to paint another one just like it, but in different colors. Were they crazy? Each painting is a one-of-a-kind. I couldn't recreate one again if I tried...and I have tried. It doesn't work for me that way. That was my first and last art gallery opening. I had too much social anxiety back then to go through another round. My, how things have changed. Life does get better.

I have thought about putting my paintings and photos on the front of of Angel Cards, greeting cards, stuff like that. Maybe I will.

Archangel Jophiel is a peaceful, joyful, and inspirational creative angel. If you have a tedious project you are working on, ask Jophiel to inspire you and to open your mind to new ideas.

Here are a few of my divinely guided pieces:

Angel in Prayer

My husband calls this one "The Pregnant Byzantine Horse"

Chapter 2 God, Angels, & Orbs

Angel Mermaid

Pegasus Angel

Garden Angel

I painted this Madonna during my birthday week in August, 1993. Pope John Paul II was in Colorado. His prayer was televised, and when the choir sang…it was heavenly. Out came my easel, and she was born.

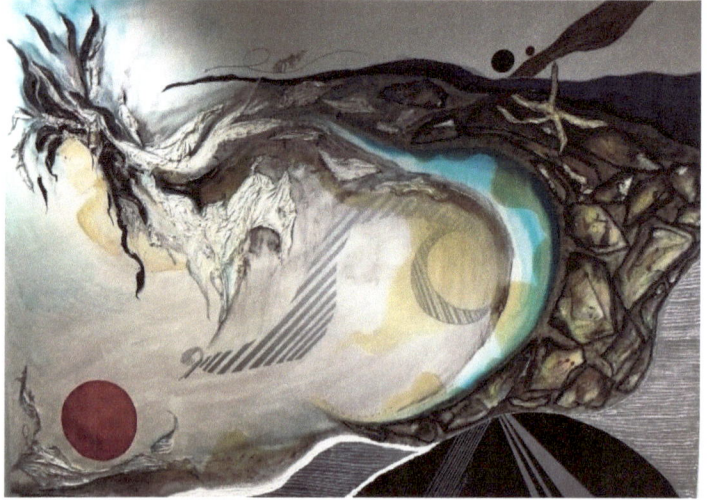

Atlantis

My version of Gustave Klimt's "The Kiss." It is actually me and my husband, Emilio. He is so handsome, it drops me to my knees!

Now I lay me down to sleep

The Agreement

Contemplation

Magic Dancers

Cairo

Chakra Angel

Life

Lemurian Haze

Connecting with Archangel Jophiel

Mind: Take a deep breath and exhale. Look around you for a simple yet thought-provoking object. Acknowledge its beauty, uniqueness, and the joy it brings you.

Body: Dear Jophiel, please help me to recognize and appreciate the beauty and creativity that surrounds me. Help me to manifest splendor in my life and in others. Thank you. Amen.

Spirit: I saw the angel in the marble and carved until I set him free.
- Michelangelo

10. Archangel Jeremiel

Jeremiel's name means "Mercy of God." In addition to being an archangel of prophetic visions, Jeremiel helps newly crossed-over souls to review their lives. He helps those still living to take an inventory of our lives so we can make positive changes for our future. Jeremiel brings assistance with visions, life reviews, psychic or prophetic dreams, and clairvoyance. Jeremiel helps us when we are having emotional or physical difficulties and teaches us to act in loving ways. He gives us courage to change our lives in a positive fashion. This in turn ends our negativity or despair and begins our healing process. Archangel Jeremiel has a blueish purple tone. This is related to the brow chakra, also called the third eye. Over the years I have had help from Jeremiel. Three prophetic events, visits, come to mind.

1. A family member owned a rental house in a pleasant neighborhood with new tenants. The renters had six children. Shortly after the tenants moved in, I dreamt that I was standing in the front yard of this house while being able to see through the walls. I was watching two of their children

closing their bedroom door and then crawling under their bunk bed. They had matches and started to light tissue paper on fire. The tissue paper soon started a larger fire under their bed. The two boys scrambled out of their bedroom, closed the door, and ran out to the backyard, telling no one. I then saw the house almost completely burned down and ambulances in the driveway. I saw badly burned children being carried out and a frantic mother. When I woke up after this "prophetic dream" my heart was pounding. I called the owners and told them I was worried that the tenants' kids would start a fire that day. I explained that I'd had a dream and that the fire marshal would be calling around lunchtime with bad news. I asked them to please check on the tenants and talk to the parents. They laughed at me and said I was crazy. Around dinnertime my phone rang, and it was the owner of that rental house. They wanted me to know that the fire marshal did call them around 12:30 that the house was almost burned to the ground, and several of the tenants' children were badly burned. They told me that I must be a witch and they didn't want to hear anything else from me. I was astonished that they called me and by their complete lack of remorse. Just because they can't hear a dog whistle blowing doesn't mean someone else can't. I can. Jeremiel, thank you for the dream.

2. I was on the highway driving home from work one evening, thinking about what to make for dinner, when I got a horrible burning feeling in my throat. Then I saw in my mind's eye, one of my young twin daughters choking on a piece of fried cheese at a local restaurant. Was I nuts? They were supposed to be at home, not at a restaurant. As I was approaching the exit for this restaurant, my car went into autopilot. I drove to the restaurant, parked my car, and ran in. I knew exactly where she was sitting. There she was, her

little head on the table, choking on a piece of deep fried string cheese. The irresponsible relatives at the other end of the table didn't even notice me or her, as they were too busy having a good time. I grabbed my child and tried to free the cheese from her throat. It was already cooled and stuck in her throat. I did the Heimlich maneuver, which dislodged the cheese enough so that when I flipped her upside down, I could grab the cheese and pull it from her throat. She had blisters in her mouth and began to cry. I gathered up my girls and left the restaurant. Jeremiel, thank you for the vision.

3. One evening after a long day with many extended-family issues to contend with, I was ready to drop. Around one o'clock in the morning I found myself sitting up in bed, looking at a man dressed in late nineteenth-century clothing from Spain. He looked just like my husband but taller. He spoke to me in Spanish, though his mouth did not move. He was talking to my mind, and I understood every word he said. I was happy to see him and felt as if I knew him. I also felt great love for this man, pure joy to see him. His name was Emilio -- the grandfather after whom my husband was named. He told me much about himself. How he died, when he died in Spain, what he was wearing (which is what he had on that night), and that he was glad I had married his grandson. He also told me not to worry and that everything was going to be okay. I settled back down and closed my eyes. I did not know what to think, but I had a feeling of peace and calm. Then I felt him sit on the side of our bed and place his hand on my leg. He told me to sleep and that he would be watching over us. The next morning I mustered up the courage to tell my husband who had come to visit and what he had to say. When I told him that his grandfather had died at age forty-eight and not in his late seventies, he said I was crazy. I told him to call his mom in

Miami and ask her about everything his grandfather had told me. He called. My mother-in-law confirmed every detail, right down to the clothes he was buried in. Jeremiel, thank you for my visitor.

Spiritual visits, psychic visions, or prophetic dreams happen to many people. However, many people tend to dismiss these events as coincidence and they don't talk about them at all. I see them as an opportunity to reevaluate my priorities and my choices in life.

I appreciate Archangel Jeremiel for assisting me in these endeavors.

Connecting with Archangel Jeremiel

Mind: Visualize a blueish-purple radiant beam of light passing through your body into the earth below. Your mind is flooded with imagines and hope for the future.

Body: Dear Jeremiel, help me to review my life and make positive changes now. Please help me to trust my intuition, visions, and prophetic dreams as I implement these changes. Thank you. Amen.

Spirit: An angel can illumine the thought and mind of man by strengthening the power of vision and by bringing within his reach some truth which the angel himself contemplates.
- St. Thomas Aquinas

11. Archangel Zadkiel

Zadkiel is the most amazing shade of indigo-periwinkle purple. I have always seen him when I close my eyes, beautiful. Zadkiel's name translates as "the righteousness of God." Zadkiel helps you to find mercy, compassion, and forgiveness toward yourself and others. Zadkiel helps you to let go of judgments or being stuck in anger, sadness, or despair. He also brings calm, emotional healing, and removes negativity. He heals painful memories while at the same time enhancing an excellent memory. Two things I cherish are my unusually excellent memory skills, and the release of feeling devastating sorrow when recalling sad memories from my past.

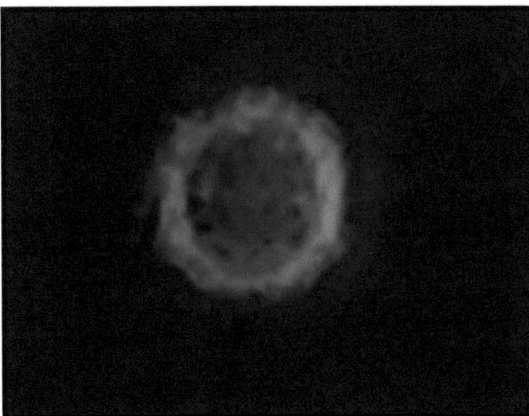

Forgiveness truly does set us free. Forgiveness is a tough and ugly pill to swallow, but is essential for us to move forward in life. I have had to forgive, just as you have had to forgive. How do you forgive the unforgivable act of another? When somebody is robbing a restaurant for a one-hundred-dollar check and puts a bullet in the head of my friend? When an aneurysm ends the life of my only childhood friend, a young pregnant mother of two? When a physician commits egregious malpractice and your child ends up on life support, facing years of reparative surgery and chronic pain? When your closest friend, "sista from a different mista," gets diagnosed with pancreatic cancer while your child is on life support? You just can't make these things up. These events were all real and they happened to me. Bad things do happen to good people. As we collapse on our knees in horrific emotional pain, these events test our faith. They also make us stronger and we survive.

If we hold on to anger, rage, disbelief, or self-blame, our energy affects others around us. I cannot force the earth to spin out of orbit any more than I can control the actions of another. We are all born with free will, and we all make choices every day. We can raise our vibration of love and find peace and grace or we can stay stuck in the pain and sadness of troubling events.

When someone chooses to do harm, that is their free will. They will have to reconcile their actions with their own soul and God, not with me, not with you. I have learned that no matter what I could have done or said, it would not have changed or stopped any of these events. But my reaction to an event -- my feelings, my mindset, and prayer -- *can* effect change with the aftermath. What I do to affect the outcome of a devastating event is to help heal the souls left behind, to give immense love to those as they pass, and to forgive those who harm others, intentionally or not. I pray for them, I ask for a miracle to heal the event, I ask for forgiveness for myself and others, and then I visualize them in God's divine light.

I have also learned that I cannot change the contracts that other souls have with God concerning their life, timing, or way of death. I believe before our souls are born into a physical body we sign up for life lessons with God. These "lessons" are our contracts and agreements while on Earth. God is the only one who can modify our

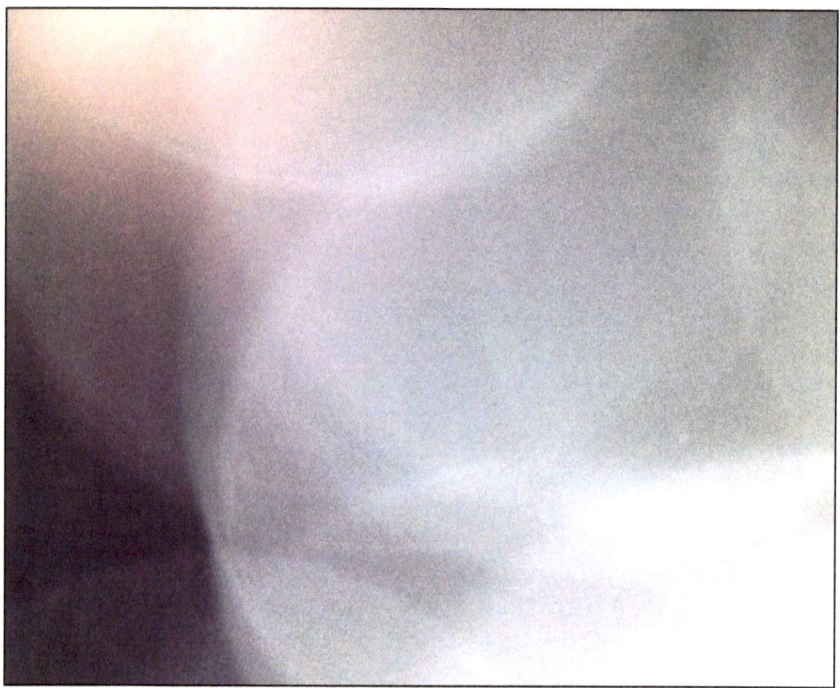

contract, only if we ask, and only if it is in our highest and best good.

Chapter 2 God, Angels, & Orbs

I have learned that asking God to take me and spare my child's life almost happened. Our child was "crashing" again and needed more blood, and more surgery to save her life. The doctors immediately sent me to donate two pints of blood for her. When we arrived back at the hospital from the blood donation center, the first bag was finished and they were hanging the second bag of my blood. I felt relieved, that maybe my blood going into my child's body would help her soul feel safe, that she would stay, and not die that day. My husband and I left the hospital around 10:00 pm to run home and shower. Two of our other children were with her; we never left her alone at the hospital. We would then head back to her side in the ICU. I was on the phone with the ICU nurse for a few minutes around 10:30 pm when I got up from my desk to tell my husband that I was going to skip the shower, and that we needed to get back to the hospital right away. As I got up and took a few steps from my desk I felt a tremendous pain in my heart. I had experienced issues with my heart ever since I was a little kid. This time I had no warning sign, but somehow I knew it was going to be really bad. Then I thought for a split second that this was the end. I was about to die.

No one could quite figure out what was wrong with me -- why I fainted at the most unusual times, or why I had chest pain and heart palpitations. One time on the farm, when I was about thirteen years old, I passed out while baling hay. The adults said I was looking for attention or that I was pregnant. They drove me to the local doctor and ordered a blood test for pregnancy. Of course it was negative, as it would have been impossible, unless it was an immaculate conception. Those adults then decided that I just didn't want to bale hay, so back into the field I went.

This time, the next thing I discerned was that the carpet pattern on the stairs was really beautiful; I was happy with my carpet selection. I also wondered why my face was smashed on the carpet at the bottom of our lengthy spiral staircase. As my heart was kicking back in I vomited as I usually do after an episode. I was so relieved to be alive. I tried to lift my arm, but it wouldn't move. I lay there crumpled like a sad sack of meat. In fact, I couldn't move any part of my body and everything hurt. When the paramedics arrived, they strapped me to a board and carted my sorry butt up the stairs, out of our house, and into an ambulance. I was off for an adventurous and painful ride to the cardiac ward in the same hospital where our child was on life support. My poor husband. Our entire world was falling apart. The ambulance driver told my husband that they would not run the siren or the lights unless something serious happened during the ride. They told him to follow the ambulance to the hospital. I prayed in the ambulance to keep him strong. I felt like such a loser. Unfortunately, during that ride I had another episode. On went the lights and the sirens. I can't believe my husband didn't have a heart attack himself.

A few weeks later I had cardiac ablation, and the procedure worked. Bazinga! That was a good thing.

What did l have to learn? As I lay in my bed in the cardiac ward I sobbed myself silly. The nurses kept coming in to check on me because my monitors kept going off. My child, my friend with cancer, and I were the Three Amigos at our healing practice. How could all of these horrible events happen to all of us within six weeks? The previous five years had not been easy, but were also filled with many wonderful things. However, my sister had a brain tumor; my twins had several spinal fusions (I blamed myself for their bone issues, and not being able to carry them to full term); my husband had neck fusion (I should have known); and this list goes on and on, "Shoulda," "coulda," "woulda," everything was supposed to be under my control, right? I thought I was supposed to prevent or fix everyone and everything. I was supposed to make everyone's life perfect, pain free, easy. That was my goal, my job, and I thought my life purpose. Is anyone thinking ... "Control Freak?" I wanted to protect, fix, and paint their worlds better than mine. Why should they feel pain when I had enough for everyone? I absolutely didn't and don't want to control them. I simply wanted to renegotiate their contract with God. My plan blew up in my face. I was a mess. I couldn't even help myself. Just brilliant.

I'd honestly thought I was done with the horrific hurdles from above. Had I really signed up for this? Didn't I try hard enough? Wasn't I good enough? What else did God want from me? How could I have screwed up so much that I somehow allowed others to suffer? What happened to my "Magical Unicorn Powers" of protecting others from harm?

I did not sleep one wink that night; I just prayed. I talked to God and asked him to send more Angels, to forgive my sorry example of a

Chapter 2 God, Angels, & Orbs

human being. I could not do it by myself anymore. *I give up, I quit, I don't want to be a Lone Wolf anymore, and I told God I am obviously not the Wonder Woman I had convinced myself I was.* I would be of no help to our daughter if I were dead. I would be of no help to my sister/friend/office manager with pancreatic cancer if I were dead. I would be of no help to my husband and our other children if I died.

I had to start to forgive the incompetent doctor whose horrific and careless conduct put our child in the ICU on life support. I had to forgive things I had no control over. I had to forgive myself for not being able to save Henry from his fatal gunshot or SHL from her fall. I had to forgive my unavailable biological family. I had to forgive myself for not being a super hero.

As the sun started to rise, it barely peeked through the window and fashioned a soft golden glow in the room. In walks my primary care doctor. Mr. Einstein Brain. I was a little embarrassed about my bruised, scraped-up face and limbs, and my unbelievably pathetic situation. However, I was very happy and surprised to see him. (By the way, his actions and care are the reason our child did not die from her injuries. He got every specialist known to man to work on her.) A few minutes later two cardiologists came in to tell me what the plan was going to be to fix me. They said I needed to take medication before my surgery, as my issue was now life-threatening. That surprised me because I was actually feeling better. I had to laugh when they rattled off a few medication suggestions. Then they said, "How about digitalis"? They said that it came from foxglove, so I should be happy with it, since I was a naturopath/homeopath. I said great. "Digitalis it is!" I then told the physicians a story about wild mustangs accidentally eating naturally growing foxglove. The mustangs had been transplanted to an area with this deadly plant. I told them the horses died, and it took the government a while to figure out their mistake. They eyed me with utter disbelief. Apparently I had grown the two heads out of my neck again, just like when I was younger. Silly me, I thought they might like to hear a fun fact about digitalis in light of the situation we were talking about.

I signed the discharge papers, got up, and looked for my clothes so I could go down the elevator to the ICU and be with my child. Bummer -- I had come by ambulance in only my girlie underpants and a small t-shirt. BAZINGA (love that word), in walks my sister with some clothes. Things were looking up. My attitude and spirit had been lifted. I had hope again and a much clearer picture of my purpose. Apparently heaven just needed to adjust my attitude the hard way.

Zadkiel is truly one of my buddies. He helped me with the unforgiveable and move forward. When you are faced with a seemingly insurmountable event, just call him. He always answers his phone.

Connecting with Archangel Zadkiel

Mind: Turn your palms up and rest them on your lap. Surround yourself in radiant purple light. Breathe a sigh of relief as you remember how it felt to be truly forgiven for a past mistake.

Body: Dear Zadkiel, please help me to forgive myself and all people involved in the life lessons that have caused me pain, sorrow, and despair. Help me move forward with love and acceptance, as it is not my place to pass judgement. Please help me find mercy and surround all in Heaven's light. Thank you. Amen.

Spirit: We go to the grave of a friend saying, "A man is dead," but angels throng about him saying, "A man is born."
- Henry Ward Beecher 1813 – 1887

Chapter 2 God, Angels, & Orbs

12. Archangel Azrael

Azrael is a lovely creamy mist-colored orb. Azrael's name means "Whom God helps." Azrael's role is primarily to cross people over to heaven at the time of physical death. Azrael comforts people prior to their physical death, ensures they do not suffer during death, and helps them to embrace heaven. Azrael gives support and comfort during grief and assists the newly crossed-over soul. Compassion, peace, transition, and comfort. Azrael is also the patron Angel of the clergy.

This photo was taken the day Patricia, my friend with pancreatic cancer, left for heaven. We were in a small village in Mexico on the Sea of Cortez. There were no flights back to the U.S. We were stuck there for three more very long days.

I was very grateful that I was able to tell her I loved her over the phone. Her family held the phone up to her ear at the hospital. When she heard me, she smiled and said "Spock?" She always called me "Spock," or the "Wizard" from *The Wizard of Oz*.

The last time I'd seen her I knew it would be my last. She knew this as well. When I'd gone to her home a few weeks earlier, the sun was shining. I smiled as I walked into her kitchen. She had made over one hundred yummy cupcakes with bright Bronco-orange frosting. Her house smelled great. I sat on a stool at the island in her kitchen. I asked her what was up with the cupcakes. She said she wanted to make over one hundred cupcakes to prove she could do it, so she did. She was also listening to Bono and Bruce Springsteen. She asked me if I liked the music she was playing. I did. She then told me that she wanted this music played at her funeral. I was so overcome with shock, internal grief, and sadness that I couldn't speak, so I just listened. She went on to tell me that she wanted Mardi Gras beads of different colors for people to wear at her service. She wanted a party and not a "funeral." She shared so much with me and asked me my opinion on everything, down to her wanting people to wear beach attire and flip-flops. I agreed with every wish and thought that she shared.

Patricia then told me that the home health care nurse would not give her the injections she needed that day because the box of drugs delivered had her husband's name on the outside. She wanted to get her blood cell count up so she could do yet another round of chemo. She wanted to make it until her youngest daughter graduated from high school in May. I gave her every injection right then and there, standing by her cupcakes, as she requested.

We talked for many more hours. I realized her soul was already half gone. It was now getting dark and snowing like a monster. She needed to rest so I told her I had to leave, but that I would be back. I am sure she could read the look on my face. I wanted to cry. She was so weak, pale, and skinny, yet she opened the cupboard door to grab a jar of the baby food I had recommended for her; she said they tasted good. She then smiled at me so lovingly, her complete soul was present at this moment. She thanked me for her job, changing her life, being such a good friend, and loving her like a sister. I couldn't speak, even though I tried. I thought of how she had stayed by my daughter's bedside while she was on life support, until I could get there. Words could never thank her enough; all three of our souls have been and forever will be connected. We were the Three Amigos – "No man left behind" -- that was our motto at the office.

I kissed her cheek, gazed at her beautiful face, hugged her, and opened the front door. We both knew this would be the last time I would see her on Earth. As soon as I closed the front door, my tears fell like a waterfall. I cleaned the snow off my car, got in, and drove down the block. I parked my car and sobbed for what seemed an eternity. I don't cry. I don't want to cry. I pride myself on not crying.

Nothing I could do would stop the river of tears. My drive home was so sad. Every song on the radio was about angels, death, or loss. I would not trade that day with Patricia for anything in this world. I miss her so much. I feel her presence all the time. I say good morning to her and talk to her every day on my way to our office. Though she loved the Pope and had a picture of him taped to our front desk, I placed an angel statue on our patio at the office for her. She could hang with us any time she wants, and she does.

When we lose a loved one it is beyond devastating. Life will never be the same; it will be different. Even the tough ones have to pick themselves up and appreciate the joy and grace of their gift of being in our lives. This is what I do with the help of God and heaven's Angels.

After Patricia left for her new assignment in heaven, I took this photograph of her spirit at a special performance of the Colorado Ballet in her honor. I was talking to her and asked her to show up. Patricia was a beautiful ballerina and dancer when she was younger. She also loved the ocean and called herself the "Mountain Mermaid," so cool. Patricia is still a ballerina and an Angel in heaven.

A year after her passing I was at a conference where John Holland (world respected psychic medium) was speaking about mediumship and life after death. There were over 1,100 people in the audience. My youngest daughter and I were in the very back of the room. John Holland decided to do three audience readings at the end of his lecture. He gave his first two readings, which were astounding. Then he said he had a ballerina twirling around calling out for "the wizard." He said this message was for a person in the back of the room and this person had Angels everywhere in their office. I stood up with my daughter as they put a mic in my hand. He had us come to the front of that conference room and gave us the most heartfelt messages from Patricia. She also wanted me to tell her husband that she will always love him.

Patricia had planned to attend these conferences with us. Life had changed so quickly. Her plate was full, as heaven had other plans for her. But look who came to this conference all on her own!

Thank you, Azrael, for being with and helping my sis.

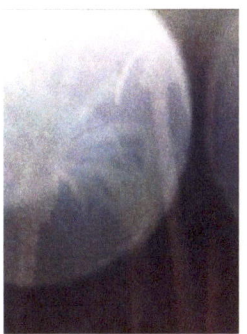  

Connecting with Archangel Azrael

Mind: Relax all muscles in your body. Wiggle your fingers and toes, breathe life in, exhale and renew. Surround yourself in an enormous soft and fuzzy ball of buttercream colored light.

Body: Dear Azrael, please comfort me and be with my loved one as they transition and return to Heaven. Please ease my sorrow, release my fear, and be with me when my time comes. Thank you. Amen.

Spirit: Perhaps they are not stars, but rather openings in heaven where the love of our lost ones pours through and shines down upon us to let us know they are happy.
-Eskimo Proverb

13. My Guides

Do you see colors when you close your eyes? I do. Have you ever gone to bed, closed your eyes, and you could still see? Crazy stuff, but true. I am not talking about an eye-brain imprint of what you just saw. This is not like seeing a reflected image in your brain after staring at a lightbulb. No, I do not have a brain tumor, mental condition, or a medical problem that needs to be checked out. Well, I take that back; you may have to confirm my issues with my husband!

As a kid I would open and close my eyes in the dark to see if I could still see my friends. I could. When we close our eyes in a dark room it should be dark. When I close my eyes during day or night, I look to the front between my eyebrows. At first it looks like sparkles and then it turns into clouds of color moving around, much like a mist-filled lava lamp. The colors change and can turn into faces, my next painting in three dimension, vivid pictures, words, or detailed thoughts. I thank my guides for being with me and ask them to stay with me throughout the day and night.

We all have guardian angels and guides assigned to us for our life's journey. Have you ever thought about your favorite color and why you like it? Try searching the internet and type in "angels and their colors." Read about the different associations and then meditate or say a prayer, asking the angel to be with you and guide you through your day. Eventually you will learn what resonates with you and it will become habit.

Have you ever found a penny or coin in the most unusual place? I can walk out of my office and walk back in, only to find a dime in the middle of the floor. I also find dimes by my car door, on the counter, in the grass, and in some really odd places. I can just be standing someplace, like at the airport. I once bent over to check my luggage tag and get my ticket from the lower front pouch. I gave the baggage guy my ticket, he checked me in, I bent down to put my ticket back in my carry-on bag, and bazinga, there sits a shiny new dime.

Guides and Angels give us signs all the time. We just have to pay attention to little things. I was sitting on the beach in Mexico, reading a book. A huge and I mean really huge, purple butterfly flew up in front of my face. It fluttered there for about thirty seconds.

Then it gracefully flew off over the ocean, staying the same size, and disappeared. I looked around me at the other people and no one had noticed it. How could they not see a butterfly the size of a grapefruit? Well, it was meant for me. I took this photo about an hour later. The weather was calm, warm, and dry. There was no precipitation, just a beautiful day. I had lots of friends with me that day on the beach.

I have physically felt or seen my guides on many occasions. I have names or colors for them. My dear friend and psychic medium, Rebecca Rosen, helped me with some of their specific names. The rest of them, well, I just knew.

We all have guides to help us throughout our lives. Guides can be with us for a lifetime or come and go as we need them.

Butterfly, Feather, Rue, Mr. Buffalo, Peach, Athena, Transmutation, Mr. Electric, and Calle, are all part of my Delightful Dozen.

1. Butterfly is a butterfly and purple in color. When I see butterflies I say a quick prayer of thanks for everything joyful

in my life. When I see a purple butterfly I am immediately covered in goose bumps. I recognize how beautiful and fragile life is and I thank God for the magnificent Earth we inhabit.

2. Feather is a feathery winged spirit. I have used feathers in my paintings ever since I was a child. I love feathers and angel wings. Victoria's Secret models have cool wings as well -- too bad they don't sell their displays! My "feather" has wings like the models wear. Sometimes on my way to work I will see wing decals on a car. After I park my car and get out, I look down, only to find a bunch of bird feathers on the ground. Then, when my first person of the day walks in with Indian feathers printed on their shirt, I take notice, smile, and tell them I like their shirt. This is a nice sign that Feather is here for the day to help me.

3. Rue is the color of rue. A peachy-beige red tone, much like the sunsets in Colorado. Rue is a color I have for some of my fall clothes. I find that when I am drawn to this color I simply want to curl up, watch a family movie, eat soup, or look at old photo albums. After looking at our photo albums, crazy stuff usually happens. Lights go on or off, the faucet in my bathroom sink turns itself on, or the phone rings from someone we have not heard from in a while. I mentally say "Hi" to our departed loved ones and light a candle in their honor.

4. Mr. Buffalo looks just like a real buffalo. In the middle of the night, I will sometimes hear a loud crash or boom sound coming from our living room. Our dogs know he is there and race out of the bedroom to bark at him. When I arrive in the living room Mr. Buffalo is standing there staring at me like nothing has happened. I thank him for coming and go back to bed. Mr. Buffalo shows up when a business or financial loose end is turning into a favorable outcome. He always brings a win-win solution or contract the very next day.

5. Peach is the color of white peach and she helps me with maternal things. I have always loved the color of white peach. Peach first showed up for me when I was in high school. I painted my bedroom this color, as it made me feel like I had a mom. My biological mother lived in another state, I rarely saw

her. My step-mother, at that time, ignored me, like I was invisible. She made sure to look past me, towards the wall, dead space, or something in the distance when I spoke to her. She rarely spoke me, unless it was an order to do something she did not want to do. She mostly pretended I did not exist. Peach was hanging with me again while our oldest twin daughter was pregnant. I was at our daughter's ultrasound when she said her baby was the size of a peach. I smiled ear to ear. I nicknamed my granddaughter Peach. We call our granddaughter "Peach" to this day.

6. Athena is "Athena" and her nickname is Trina. I painted a picture of her in January 1995. Her portrait hangs in our bedroom. This painting has a red angel orb (Metatron), streaks of silvery transparent tubes of light, clouds, and waves of water. Athena is known as the Greek goddess who fiercely protected her home, though she did not have a mother. Sounds eerily similar to me! She is the goddess of reason, intelligent activity, arts, and literature. She also brought us the bridle to tame horses. I had no idea who I had painted until many years later. I called her Athena long before I ever saw a picture of her.

7. Transmutation. Transmutation means to change the atoms of one element into another. Transmutation hangs with me on the days that things do not turn out as I had planned. He seems to show up when I have my heels dug in and want something in a particular way. The next thing I know my hard headedness has gone out the window and I go with the new plan. It usually is something much better.

8. Mr. Electric is responsible for my delightful sense of electrical shock and the occasional ability to turn on lights without a switch. When Spirit shows up and I am not paying attention to my guides or angels, he gives me a zap. Example: During an appointment at the office I was helping a gal with recent weight gain, digestive issues, and anxiety. She swore she had no other issues and didn't know why these problems had started. I then received an electrical zap shooting out of my right toes that made my leg jerk and my toes sting. I asked her if she had a problem with her right foot or toes. She frowned at me, as if I was not listening to her complaints properly.

However, she bent over and took off her winter UGG boots. She showed me her blistered, mangled hammer toes and told me she was supposed to have surgery to fix them, but didn't. She told me they had gotten much worse in the past months and it was hard for her to walk.

She had spent the last several months sitting on her couch, eating lots of junk food, becoming constipated from taking pain pills for her feet, worrying about her increasing weight, and ignoring the underlying reason for her current condition. Mr. Electric is excellent at helping me "feel" someone's pain to find the underlying cause of their issues. If she had taken the advice to fix her foot, the snowball would not have turned into a snowman. I am happy to report that all is well; she got the surgery, her toes are fixed, and she is back to a happy and healthy gal.

Mr. Electric likes to play with electricity. May 27, 1995 -- Our three girls have the same birth date, so preparations for their birthday party always takes a few days. One year my husband was busy in the backyard putting together a huge tent for them to play in with the neighborhood kids. Once the tent was up we were going to paint it with flowers, animals, their names, and more. I was in the house, cleaning, and my handsome husband was wrestling this monster tent project by himself in 100-degree weather. I went outside to check on him and see if he wanted some help. He declined as the sweat dropped from him. I went back into the house to finish cleaning. When I walked into our master bedroom the ceiling overhead light came on. I thought that was weird but dismissed it. But as I walked into the master bath, I noticed the light in our bedroom went off. Now I was curious. I went back into the master bedroom, and as I walked toward the light it got brighter. I couldn't believe what was happening. I felt tingly and had goose bumps from head to toe. I raised my hands to the light and it got extremely bright. When I put my hands down the light dimmed. I practically leaped out of the bedroom just to see what would happen next. The light went off.

I repeated this exercise a dozen times. I was so shocked that I ran downstairs, outside, and stood directly in front of my husband, who was covered in sweat and still struggling with the tent. I almost wet my pants telling him what had happened and that I needed him to come inside so I could show him. He was not impressed, nor pleased with this request. However, he eventually came inside to appease me.

When I showed him what was happening he said I was messing with him, he didn't have time for this, and that I had a remote control or something in my pocket to change the light. I did not. He checked the wall switches and the remote for the fan. All were off. I asked him to walk into our bedroom, toward the light, raise his hands, and see if it would light up. It did not light up for him. When I walked into our room, the light came on and got brighter and brighter. We both stepped out of the bedroom and tried this exercise again and again. The light turned on and got brighter every time I walked into the room and raised my hands. He said he had no logical explanation. I had an explanation. It was Mr. Electric letting me know he was with me. I also wondered if the inventor of "Clap On-Clap Off" had a similar experience!

9. Calle. Calle is my writing guide. She helps me find my words and thoughts. In Spanish, "Calle" means road or pathway. How appropriate that she is leading me through such a lovely path of writing! She floods my brain with pictures, memories, and inspiration. Many times there is so much information that I am not sure that I can organize every detail hours later. But, all that I have to do is focus and ask that she rematerializes the thoughts and pictures when I am at my desk. Within a few moments, Bingo! What a wonderful guide!

10. My Delightful Dozen. We all have guides. Sometimes we have one or two. Sometimes we collect them to help us with various tasks. I like to invite as many as I can from different vocations. When I play the piano I mentally ask Bach, Mozart, or another composer, to sit with me and guide me. I don't play like they could, but I am sure I play better when they are with me. When I have a complex problem I ask Einstein to help me think out of the box. Other days I am drawn to a particular color or crystal. Everything I run into that day seems to be that color. I have pondered many times about the color and the issue I was dealing with that day; they

always go together. Not all guides have names. They appear as colors as well. It is amazing to reflect on whatever issue you may be dealing with, the color you see all day long, and the answer about how to handle your concern.

Here are some of my color experiences:

Green/Jade: Get up. Get going, start something, steadily take action. I start and finish a project I have been putting off.

Orange/Coral: Take a breather, take a chill pill, go with the flow, it will all work out. I keep my mouth shut, listen, and if it is not life-threatening, I let it go.

Purple/Violet: I need to balance my Mind, Body, & Spirit. Something is amiss, and I need to take care of myself. I take a salt bath, paint, pray, or meditate. I ask God and the Angels to assist me.

Turquoise: I may need to communicate difficult information with more empathy, zero judgment, all while trusting my intuition on the issue. I pay very close attention to what Spirit shares with me. I communicate the information gently and exactly as I was shown, then I shut up. I let the person process it and they then solve their own dilemma. They are empowered when I get out of the way and remove my human ego.

Brown/Auburn: I need healthy boundaries today, something to ground me. Earthy dense foods are usually what I eat on these days, and I usually wear flats and a sweater. A step or a walk outside and a deep breath is a good way to ground yourself.

Pink/Rose: I need to send love, trust my intuition, connect with others, and give someone a hug. This is an easy day, and I find that I get a lot of hugs and good tidings in return. Lead with love because we all need love.

Blue/Sapphire: I need to protect and regenerate my energy. If my pitcher is empty I have nothing to offer. When I know I have a tough day ahead, I wear some shade of blue. I imagine heaven's blue light energizing and healing me so I can move through my day calmly and with intention.

Red/Ruby: I will have a day full of passion, accomplishment, inspiration, and more energy. These are days that I get so much done. I feel like a ferret who drank six cups of coffee. The energy comes from the inside and expands out. I go from sunup to sundown, doing everything I can think of. This is when my husband says to "calm down." I don't have an excess of red days, thank goodness.

Black/Gray: I need to clear my energy and rest. Sleep is a good thing. I need to look for what I am missing, go inside myself, and find the answer. Sleeping and dreaming does the trick for me.

Pearly Silver/White: I need to connect to Source, clear my mind, raise my vibration, and listen to what heaven is sharing with me. I can be a better channel of love, light, and healing when I surround myself and others in this color. I find that praying in the shower is a great place to cleanse, clear, and envelop everyone I love in this color. A great way to start the day.

Yellow/Gold: I need to follow through on a creative idea and think outside the box. I write down my ideas and then go back to them and expand my thoughts until I am satisfied. When this is complete, I put my thoughts into action.

Multicolor: I need to go back to my happy inner child and smile. I need to do something crazy, funny, or quirky. Now that our children are grown, my husband or my staff is usually the target of my playfulness or goofiness. Poor things.

You get the picture. For decades I have witnessed that people wear or are drawn to certain colors depending on what their issues are and how they are feeling. My guides have pointed this out to me clearly and my experience has proven it.

Connecting with Your Guides

Mind: Breathe in vibrant colored light and reenergize your soul. Smile, because this party is about you.

Body: Dear Guides, please be with me and bring me a sign of your presence. Help me to quickly and accurately comprehend your message. Flood my mind with great ideas and guide me to my greatest potential. Thank you. Amen.

Spirit: We're all kissed by angels but some of us never think to pucker.
-Unknown

3 HUMAN ANGELS

If anyone ever tells you that they had a perfect childhood, I wonder if they've been watching a 1950s television show. No one has perfect parents, or a perfect life with no problems. I used to think that the other kids I knew had so much more than I did. I was happy for them, yet I couldn't understand why I didn't live in their world. They must be very blessed and really good children, I figured, so they really deserved it. But as it turned out, God had other plans for me, and for those "good" children as well, including my best friend SHL.

Jesus, being a son of God, would be the only one I can think of who had a perfect parent. Yet his life was filled with pain, according to scripture. Why didn't his father protect him from pain and suffering? Why do we have parents who do not or cannot protect us from pain and suffering? These are all very good questions. In my mind, tragedy finds us all to different degrees, based on what we can handle. Tragedy is also a perspective. When we lose a loved one, it can bring us to our knees. When we hear of someone we did not know losing a loved one, we are sorry for them and go about our lives. We bring them food, send a card, talk about how sad it is, and then forget about it. There are many songs about how "nobody knows the trouble I've seen." Well, we are all in this together and there is a lesson to learn on this topic.

From a very young age I knew that I would lose loved ones. It was my greatest fear, next to frogs, and the thought of eating beets. I always felt that I shouldn't get close to anyone, because they would die and I wouldn't be able to save them. Be careful what you wish for and what you fear, because both will draw near.

Chapter 3 Human Angels

My closest and best friend, SHL, was like a sister to me. She was my family. SHL and her mom taught me not to wear sticky old red nail polish from the dime store, even if it was what I could afford. SHL and her mom, Mary, bought me a taupe/rose-colored polish by Maybelline. I was floored that someone was thinking of me and took the time to buy me a present. Crazy, right? It was beautiful and dried to a smooth un-gloppy finish. So uptown! SHL would always include me in her adventures. I would walk down the side country road to the main road by the pond, and she would be there waiting for me in her brother T's green two door car. It was cool, like what the *"Dukes of Hazzard"* drove. T was a bit older than SHL and me. He was tall, dark, handsome, and very smart. I always felt so "popular and special" riding in that car. What a doorknob, dork, or "Sheldon" I was. I guess I still am!

When SHL went to visit her grandma B at the nursing home after school, I would go as well. We would go on Thursdays after school, the day they served meatloaf. I would go in and say "Hi," then head back out to wait in the car, and do homework. Thirty minutes later SHL would come bounding out with a to-go plate. I always knew that SHL didn't want me to feel like a charity case. She sent me back to the car so she could spend alone time with her grandmother. I had meat loaf, mashed potatoes, canned peaches, and peas every Thursday. I figured Grandma B did not like meatloaf, so she would send it with SHL for me. That was really a great thing for her to do and for me to experience. It didn't take me long to finally ask her if I should bring her grandmother something else to eat, since she went without dinner on Thursdays because I was eating her meatloaf. SHL looked at me with huge eyes and called me a "dummy." She told me that her grandmother loved the meatloaf and always ordered another meal for me.

It fascinated me how much she cared for everyone else. She used to tell me that she wished she was smarter, that maybe she was not trying hard enough, and that she could do better. I thought she was perfect, and I wanted to be like her.

Dinner at her house was magical. We set the table while her mom made us the daily after-school snack -- Beaumonde seasoning mixed with sour cream and mayo, with a side of fresh sliced vegetables to scoop it up with. I learned that knife blades were always turned toward the plate (different than what King Henry the

Chapter 3 Human Angels

Eighth did for his wives on their last night), and the milk glass is only filled to one inch below the rim. Once, I filled my glass to the very top and drank it down, then filled it up again to the top. SHL's mom kindly asked me why I did that. I felt like a moron, but I answered her truthfully. At my house I couldn't have more than one glass of anything other than water. She told me that I could always have as much as I wanted or needed at their house. I could refill my glass, what a concept! Just don't fill it so full that I spilled it on the floor. I learned many lessons from that amazing family. I also appreciated the fact that even though I looked like a lost raccoon, they saw past that and loved me anyway.

As time went by SHL and I had many cool adventures together, and then it was time to graduate from high school. Everyone was going on a graduation trip to someplace wonderful. I had no plans and no money for a trip. She invited me to join her at her aunt and uncle's place in Fort Lauderdale, Florida. I said yes. As an employee's dependent, I had an airline pass that I could use to fly for just over five dollars. That was my plan. I caught a bus to Minneapolis/St. Paul, went down to the crew area, and waited until there was an open jump seat on a flight to Fort Lauderdale. Just before takeoff, paying passengers showed up late. My seat was gone. A pilot on his way home boarded with one of his crewmembers to take the remaining two seats. When he realized that I was by myself, he asked the other crewmember to let me have his seat. Now I was sitting in the first row of the plane with this older gentleman in his captain's uniform. I decided to keep my mouth shut and not talk to him, other than to thank him for my seat. Halfway into the flight he started to ask me questions. Did I have luggage, where was I staying, and with whom?

I almost choked, paralyzed with fear. I did not have any luggage, just the plastic grocery bag in my hand with a few items of clothing. I did not have a place to stay, as my intent was to get there a day or so early so I could figure out what bus I needed and how I was going to find SHL's relative's house before she arrived. My plan was to sleep at the airport, on a bench, or on the beach.

It did not take long before he figured out I was all alone without a dime to my name or a pot to piss in.

He was very nice to me and told me about his wife, and his two sons who were also pilots. He told me that they had lost a daughter when she was an infant. He told me his wife was a ballerina and had always wanted a daughter. He shared his lunch with me as well.

When the plane landed he told me to follow him. I thought I was going to jail or something. He picked up the crew phone on the wall in the airport and called his wife. He told her that he was bringing home a young guest to say a night or two. He told her he loved her and we would be home soon. He led me to the brand new, bing-cherry-colored Cadillac that he had parked in the garage. The aroma of the new leather was something I had never smelt before. I just sat with my plastic bag in my lap and said nothing.

As we drove along I noticed how beautiful the sky was and how massive the palm trees were. We pulled into the lower level of a very tall high-rise on the intercostal waterway. We rode an elevator to the top floor, where the doors opened up to a penthouse with ceiling-to-floor glass and breezy flowing sheers. His wife was absolutely beautiful. After she hugged and kissed him hello, she turned to me and hugged me. I froze. She then asked me to follow her to a guest bedroom. She had clothes for me, pajamas, shampoo, and towels, all laid out on the bed. She told me they were taking me to their favorite place for dinner, so to shower and get ready. In the guest bathroom, I opened the shower door, where lurked the largest Jurassic-Park creepy bug I had ever seen. To me, it looked like a cockroach the size of a kitten. I shrieked in alarm and ran to get her. She simply told me that in Florida they have water beetles and they like to come inside. She picked it up with a tissue, walked out onto their balcony, and set it free. I took my shower, all the while watching for something horrible to crawl out of the drain and kill me. I survived the shower and got dressed.

When we arrived at the Mexican restaurant we were greeted by the owner. We were seated in the middle of the packed restaurant, at their favorite table. The manager signaled for three gentlemen with sombreros and guitars to come over. The pilot asked me what song I wanted to hear. I froze again. I had never hired someone to sing to me before. He told them what to play, and it was great. I felt very lucky and also very stupid for not knowing how to act. I watched, observed, kept my mouth shut, and soaked up every detail that night.

The next morning his wife gave me a beach bag full of clothing, suntan lotion, and a hat. She told me we were going to spend the day on the boat. Cool! But why would I need a beach bag just to sit in a

Chapter 3 Human Angels

boat? I assumed the boat was a motorized aluminum fishing boat. I was so wrong. They had their own yacht.

I followed every instruction the pilot and his wife gave me. I was in heaven, on the ocean, being looked after by two angels. I learned that a greyhound is not just a dog, but a delicious vodka and grapefruit cocktail. If you put salt on the rim, it becomes a Salty Dog. They let me have one small drink, and then back to the virgin variety…salted rim, ice, grapefruit juice.

I felt so free and safe. The world was my oyster, and I had two new friends! What an incredible adventure and graduation trip I was having after all.

The next morning would be the end of this journey. The pilot was going to drive me to SHL's aunt and uncle's place after breakfast.

When we drove up to SHL's relatives' house, he paused a moment and then told me he was going to wait and watch me until I was let in. I think he wanted to *make sure* that I was not lying to him. Why would I lie to him? I am not a liar -- never have been and never will be. I had told him the truth about my predicament from the beginning. But I guess my story and how I got to Florida was pretty unbelievable, so who am I to judge? Maybe he thought I was a runway. He then reached into his crisply ironed shirt pocket and pulled out some money wrapped in a small piece of notepaper. He pressed it in my hand and said for me to take it. He told me how happy he and his wife had been with my visit. He reminded me that they had lost their baby daughter. He said that the past days had brought great joy to his wife. And then he told me she was very sick. I had known she was dying as soon as I met her; I could feel it. He said their address and phone number was on the paper and that I should call them and let them know that I made it home after my visit with SHL. He told me his wife never went out without him anymore and that she would answer the phone.

It was made very clear to me that after graduation I was expected to leave and not return. I never told them that *I really had no place to go home to*, but I promised I would call them.

My time that weekend with SHL and her aunt and uncle was straight out of *Father Knows Best*, the old black-and-white television show where everything has a place and time to happen. We went to their pool, ate sandwiches her aunt had packed for us, drank pop, and ate cookies. The next day we went to the beach. We talked about life and what we were going to do with ourselves in the future. She wanted to be an early elementary school teacher, get married, and have three children. I wanted to be an astronaut, artist, architect, or engineer, and a doctor. I didn't know how I could possibly make my dreams come true, but I had to try. She believed in me and said I could do anything I set my mind to. She always thought more of me than I did of myself.

Our weekend came to an end Sunday afternoon. SHL was staying for another week with her relatives and could not join us on the ride to the airport, and back to my reality. The ride to the airport was uncomfortably quiet. Her uncle was a nice man, but very "closed" and really never spoke to either of us. When we reached the airport he only said, "Okay, here you go," and that was it. I got out of the car, thanked him, closed the car door, and watched him drive away.

When my plane landed back in Minnesota I called the pilot's phone number from the crew lounge in the lower level of the airport. The phone rang and rang, no answer. I got an overwhelming sense of sadness as I hung up the wall phone, as if someone had just died. I wondered if his wife had passed away and couldn't answer the phone. I never called them back, I was too afraid of what I might hear. I said a prayer for both of them as I headed up the stairs to the terminal where "real passengers" traveled. I got on a city bus and contemplated what to do with myself.

I thought about SHL and how grateful I was for her love, generosity, and friendship. SHL wanted to become a teacher and was bound for college at the end of the summer. She had always known what she wanted to do with her life. I admired her.

I thought about what needed to be my first course of action. I had to buy a car. I worked my butt off hand shucking corn and baling hay by day, and bartended every night. My plan worked and it only took me about ten days to reach my goal. I bought an old burgundy-colored Pontiac coupe for five hundred dollars. Perfect.

I returned to the farm to pack my bags and my collect belongings. Funny how everything I owned in this world fit into the back seat. My next step was to begin the long road trip to the university where I had enrolled for summer classes. This strategy would provide food, education, and shelter during the summer months. This was a good plan.

My observations about other kids being very blessed while I was

Chapter 3 Human Angels

growing up were spot on. However, my assumption that I was all alone in the world was totally off the mark. I had Human Angels all around me, looking out for my every step. My adventure to Florida showed me how normal people live. It also showed me that people could be as kind as angels.

To this day I love to take photos of angels, spirit, and orbs. These photos make me smile and take me to a place of innocence.

During a visit to Arizona I told my husband that his mom was joining us for dinner. She had passed away many years before. Not pleased, my husband said the steaks were done, that he was opening some wine, and to take my "chill pill." Well, the only thing I could do to prove it was to get a camera. So here she is…my lovely mother-in-law, watching over her son in Phoenix. And yes, she did join us for dinner.

Spirit moving across our pool in Arizona. Kitchen berm in Colorado.

Our oldest son's Angel at Christmas, who stayed with him all night.

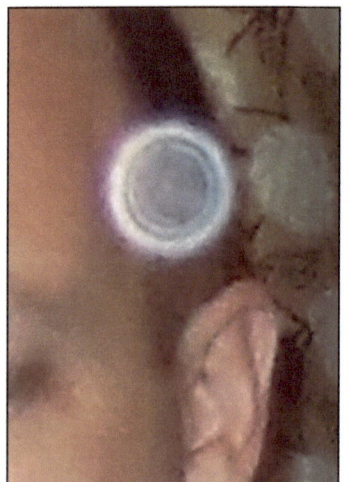

The hill by the kitchen at our home in Colorado.

Chapter 3 Human Angels

Colorado…a clear night. The fire pit and the grill were not on.

4 INTENTION & ENERGY HEALING

Almost twenty years ago I studied with one of the most kind, intelligent, and compassionate souls I would ever meet. His name was Spencer Woolley. Spencer was a brilliant classical homeopath and visionary. When he did not find people healing to his expectations he developed the BodyScan device to use both constitutional and complex homeopathic remedies thereby giving people numerous remedies in one bottle containing hundreds of frequencies. This was unheard of to traditional homeopathic doctors. Spencer's soul and mind were brilliant. He taught me much about homotoxicology, energy medicine, complex homeopathy, the energy in our cells, the fragility of the human body, and that my *intention* during healing was everything. Without *intention* I would have nothing to offer. He said I had to be *open* to receive God's healing energy so that I could serve others.

He shared a story with me one day about flying to California at the request of some parents who had a terminally ill child. He told me that the little boy was not supposed to make it through the next night. The parents were allowed to bring him home from the hospital to die in his own room. When Spencer arrived at their home late in the night, things were bleak, as the child was barely conscious and slipping away. Spencer told me that he sat at the child's bedside throughout the night, praying silently as he gave him homeopathic drops every fifteen minutes or so based on the child's symptoms -- breath, pulse, and so on. When morning came the boy opened his eyes, very weak, but still alive. The parents took him back to the hospital for further care. This child survived.

When I asked Spencer what homeopathic remedy and what potency he had given the child, he explained everything he did, why, and how, in great detail. He then told me that the homeopathic remedy stabilized and balanced the child's bodily systems. At the same time, his own personal thoughts and intentions were prayers to have God's healing energy come through him to save this young child. I was speechless. To this day, the power of intention and the power of prayer has never left my thoughts.

Intention – The Christ Light

This is a big one. Intention carries a powerful vibration that enhances healing energy. I saw his light and felt his energy as a child. This has continued throughout my life. Jesus was and is a healer; so am I. It is hard to describe the feeling of his presence. It feels like warm sun all over my body mixed with intense heat on the crown of my head, accompanied by goosebumps head to toe. When I start my day it is with a prayer. In the shower, in the car, doesn't matter.

I ask God to tell me what he wants of me for this day. I ask for Mary, Joseph, and Jesus to be with me and help me. I ask for all the

Angels to be by my side and help me. I thank my loved ones in heaven for their lives and their influence in mine. I ask that I be used as a vessel of love, light, and healing for everyone I see, to the highest and best for both them and myself. I ask that the people I see have their Angels and loved ones help me to help them heal to their best and highest good. I ask that my family and pets be blessed and protected. I ask for assistance with whatever else is on my mind. I thank them for their support, and then I thank God for my blessed life.

Our cells are energy, and they respond to energy. Think of an old lamp with a bad wiring connection. If you repair the wires, "reconnect" the wires so energy can pass through it with ease, you will be able to use the lamp your great-grandparents had, for the rest of your life.

There are many energetic modalities that stimulate healing. All modalities are enhanced by intention. If you are receiving a massage from an *"I'm in a bad mood today"* masseuse you can *feel* it. Everyone and everything is affected by energy.

Reiki, polarity therapy, Energy healing, and Hands of Light, are all energetic healing modalities. These healing techniques are based on the principle that the healer can channel energy into another person by means of touch, to activate the natural healing processes of the human body. Thus restoring physical and emotional well-being, and healing the Mind, Body, and Spirit. There are many other ways to affect the cells in our body.

Music is vibrational energy that affects our cells. We have all been taught that music can soothe the savage beast. If you have ever gone to a rock concert you can *feel* the loud, deep tones that make your heart and brain thump, while the gentle sound of a solo violin can give you goosebumps and bring you to tears. Jackie Evonco and Snatam Kaur possess human voices that give me chills and great peace simultaneously.

Vibroacoustic Therapy

Vibroacoustic Therapy (VAT) frequencies are used in vibroacoustic devices such as sound tables, loungers, mats, chairs or pillows. Vibroacoustic Therapy is a drugless, noninvasive technique addressing physical, mental, and emotional aspects, to increase the quality of our lives. The body is massaged with low-frequency vibrations, which are transmitted through the use of special transducers. The vibrations permeate the body, engaging the body to create a sympathetic resonance with the energetic frequency waves delivered.

VAT has many benefits and has been documented to stimulate blood circulation, relieve stress and anxiety, and its analgesic effect aids in pain management. It lowers blood pressure, calms the autonomic nervous system, and decreases spasms and tremors (Parkinson's, dystonia). VAT provides surface and deep tissue massage effects. It has also been found to aid with lung conditions such as asthma, COPD and cystic fibrosis. Repeated sessions have cumulative positive effects on our bodies.

Brain Waves

Our brains produce energetic frequencies such as delta, theta, alpha, beta, and gamma waves. Each of these brainwaves resonates at a different rate. Delta is between 0-4 hertz, which is used for sleeping and dreaming. Theta, between 4-8 hertz, is used for meditation, waking, falling asleep, and when our brain is on autopilot. Alpha waves are used for a calm, relaxed, and focused state between 8-12 hertz. It is the happy wave. Beta is for active learning, and we should produce 12-15 hertz for this task. Gamma waves are associated with the "feeling of being blessed" and with peak concentration and extremely high levels of cognitive functioning, like "being in the zone." Gamma waves are over 20 hertz, typically around 40 hertz.

Brainwaves are affected by sound, light, and vibration. When the brain is firing the proper frequency the body responds appropriately. It is very hard to meditate or focus standing in front of speakers and strobe lights at a Rave!

If you want to improve your brains energetic function there is an easy way to do it. Many people ask me about brain wave music or binaural music. My favorite is produced by Equisync and all you have to do is listen.

Binaural Brain Tones or Beats

Binaural beats are two tones close in hertz that generate a beat frequency from the difference of the frequencies. For example, when you transmit a 495 Hz tone to one ear and a 505 Hz tone to the other, this will produce a subsonic 10 Hz beat, about in the middle of the alpha wave range. This effect is accomplished without either ear hearing the pulse when headphones are used. Instead, the brain produces the beat by combining the two tones. Each ear hears only a steady tone. You can easily do an internet search for eocinstitute.org, or other companies, to find many helpful brain wave compilations for various conditions including sleep, meditation, relaxation, focus, and more.

Energy and Our Body

Understanding some basics about the human energy field is helpful. There are many books available about energy healing. A common theme is that we innately have this healing ability within ourselves. I agree. If we hit our elbow on something and it hurts, we immediately take our other hand and hold, rub, or soothe the injured area. We don't consciously think to do this. It just happens. We "lay our hands on" an injury and it feels better. Very simple. Imagine what you can do to heal yourself with "energy" and "intention." The laying on of hands has been used for thousands of years. Prayer, intention, and focus are all that we need.

If your mind wanders at first that is okay. The only way your mind won't wander is if you are dead. When a random thought pops into your brain, acknowledge it, and then refocus your attention back to what you are doing. This happens to all of us.

Energy healing may be easier for you to do if you use a tuning fork to help you stay focused and to get used to the sensation of vibrational healing. As you become more aware of this sensation, you may notice that you start to feel it in your hands as well. When you feel it in your hands you can also just use your hands. I use any or all modalities, depending upon the situation. Energy healing can be used for the Mind, Body, and Spirit.

For the Body:
1. Use a weighted Ohm tuning fork. Gently strike the tuning fork to start it resonating. Place the bottom end of the fork on the painful area or joint. The tuning fork will vibrate for about 15-20 seconds. Here is a neat thing to experience so you can feel and hear what is actually happening to your cells: Place your left pointer finger in your left ear canal, then strike the tuning fork to start the vibration. Place the base of the tuning fork on your left wrist bone or pointer finger knuckle. You will hear and feel what happens to the cells when vibration is used on other areas of your body.

I like to use an Ohm tuning fork on sore joints, muscles, acupressure points, and the chakras. I will repeatedly place the tuning fork on and around the affected area for about 15-20 minutes per day as needed. As you place it on the injured area you will eventually find the "sweet spot," an area that will have more sensation, and it will start to feel better.

You can use many other ranges of tuning forks. I suggest that you educate yourself about all of the many applications and varieties of tuning forks before purchasing an expensive set. You only need one Ohm tuning fork to get started.

2. Now that you can feel vibration in your body, albeit subtle, you have just taken a step toward energy healing. Hands-on healing feels very much like a tuning fork to me, but for me it includes the sensation of heat. My hands tingle, heat up, and feel as though they are vibrating from the inside out. I also develop red spots in my palms. You can use a tuning fork together with hands-on while sending healing intention. Place one hand on the body while gently grounding the tuning fork on the injured area.

Chapter 4   Intention & Energy Healing

Or you don't have to use a tuning fork for energy healing; you can just use your hands and intention. You will be able to feel the energy.

Weighted tuning forks are great to use on the body. Unweighted tuning forks are great to clear the emotional energy fields around the body. Clearing your own energy field is good for you and a must before working on anyone else. Call in your Angels and ask for Divine light to clear you.

For the Mind and Spirit:
1. I like to clear my emotional field by striking the tuning fork and starting with my crown chakra (our connection to God, Source, Divine). I move the fork in a circular motion above my head, like a spiral going up. When my arm is fully extended and I have completed my spiral, I give the tuning fork a gentle flick upwards to release any blocked energy. I visualize my "field" being cleared of fog as it lifts away. I ask for clearing and enhancement of my connection to God. I ask to be used as a vessel of love, light, and healing.
2. I then move to my brow chakra (intuition), circling the tuning fork in a small spiral motion in front of my third eye. I gradually make the spiral larger as it moves further away from my body and then give a gentle flick upwards. I ask for clarity and to "see" clearly what I need to know and what I don't understand.
3. The throat chakra is next (communication). I repeat the process of this spiraling motion as I move the tuning fork close to my throat and increase the size of the spiral as it moves away and up from my body. I ask for the ability to speak, communicate, and hear clearly with kindness.
4. The heart chakra (love) is located in the center of your chest. I repeat this spiraling process as I ask for clearing and healing of any heartache. I ask for better understanding, forgiveness, acceptance, joy, unconditional love, and harmony for myself and others.
5. The solar plexus chakra (gut decisions) is located just above your belly button. This area is where we "feel" our decisions. I ask to clear this area so I can make the best decisions based

on my "gut feelings."
6. The sacral plexus chakra is located just below your belly button (giving and receiving, family, pleasure). I spiral the tuning fork as I ask for balance in my interactions with others.
7. The base chakra (vitality, grounding, stability) is located at the base of your spine. I visualize the "fog" disappearing deep into the ground. I ask for grounding, stability, security, courage, and patience to be enhanced.
8. My final step is to spiral the tuning fork above my head and then move it down to my feet. I visualize my "field" completely clear and full of heaven's sparkly light. I visualize this "field" ten feet above my head, completely around my sides, and below my feet into the ground. It looks like a large, luminous sparkly egg-shaped energy. If I feel like I missed something, I go back and do a quick spiral in that area. I then say "thank you," "and so it is," "Amen."

This whole process takes less than five minutes. Many times during a busy day I just do a quick clearing of my energy field. This only takes ten to twenty seconds, and you don't need a tuning fork. I simply visualize a breeze of heaven's sparkly energy passing directly through my body or chakra area, clearing the fog, and then I say thank you and Amen. Think of when someone tells you to "take a deep breath" before you proceed, do something stupid, or make a decision. This is kind of the same thing. Just imagine while you take your deep breath that this sparkly healing light is filling your body with clear fresh energy. As you exhale, the fog clears and is transformed into new energy. Simple and quick. Then say "thank you" and Amen.

My best advice before engaging in an energy healing session is to set your intention to be one of pure love, healing intention, and clarity. You have to mean it and feel it. You have to truly want to help yourself or another.

Heaven will feel your intention. Ask for God, Jesus, the Angels, and your guides to be by your side and assist you. Trust me, they won't let you down.

Chapter 4 Intention & Energy Healing

Chapter 4 Intention & Energy Healing

5 CHAKRAS, COMMON MALADIES, SIMPLE STEPS FOR SELF-HEALING

Have you ever heard someone tell you to "conserve your energy or you will wear yourself out"? or "Don't waste your time, it won't work"? As the mind believes, the body will achieve. Our physical body is made up of many parts and ingredients -- water, minerals, amino acids, and so on. We need energy for life just as a vacuum cleaner needs energy to do its job. Our soul/spirit is made up of energy. Our mind/free will/ego is energy as well.

I am often asked about chakras. What are chakras and why should I care? Here is a simple explanation of what they are:

Chakras are energy points, spheres, or centers located in our energetic subtle body. The word chakra means "wheel," "circle," and "cycle." Many people describe chakras as spinning balls of energetic light. There are many chakras in the human body. Each chakra has numerous extending points, much like a lotus flower. Most people are familiar with the seven major chakras.

Why should you care? Imagine that you own a pre-lit Christmas tree with hundreds of lights. There are seven parts of your tree that need to be connected in order for all of your tree lights to sparkle. If you have a problem with a section of lights not working, your entire tree is "off." Common sense says that you go to the store to buy new lights for this "broken" or nonfunctioning section. Then, once you have repaired your tree lights, amazing things happen. You are happy, your tree is happy, everyone is happy and says what a beautiful tree you have.

Chapter 5 Chakras, Common Maladies, Simple Steps for Self-Healing

Have you ever been invited to someone's house to enjoy the holidays with spoiled hot cocoa, stale food, filthy floors, and a semi-lit Christmas tree? What would people think of that party? They would think the host of that party was a slob and cared for nothing in their life, including themselves. Nobody enjoys hanging around people, places, or things that have crappy, dull, or chaotic energy. If you are sick, people know it. They can sense and see that your energy, chi, or prana, is low and not flowing properly. The smart person who is "sick" goes home to rest and repair their energy and body. Chakras are the energy centers in our body, and they need to be cared for and attended to, just like a string of Christmas tree lights.

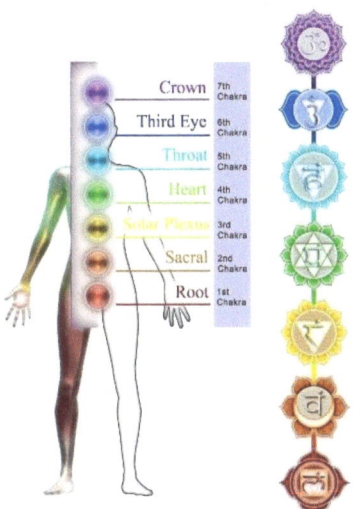

We experience many common maladies that affect us throughout our lifetimes. Most have simple repairs that we can implement before the little things spark off and become big ones, like the proverbial snowball that rolls downhill.

I have listed many of the common issues that I encounter on a day-to-day basis. My job, I believe, is to teach, educate, inform, and empower people to heal themselves. I see people for a few visits and then set them free, with the information they need for self-healing. They come back for a tune-up in six months or one year, or when life brings them a new challenge.

In health and healing there should be no judgment. Too many times I hear from people that they actually deserve or do not deserve what has happened to them. This always makes me curious. Some feel they are being punished, some are oblivious, and others feel it is a learning lesson that they want to get through. Attitude and intention play a big part in the outcome. Taking responsibility for your health is another piece of this puzzle. If you eat only fast food because you don't want to cook, or even get out of your car, you should not be surprised when you don't feel well. What we put in our body for energy will be reflected in how we feel, how clear our thinking is, our vitality.

Garbage in means garbage out. Very simple. If you feed the family dog a kid's meal from a fast food restaurant, what happens to your dog? You have a sick dog.

Life and physical death are inevitable. We all have a physical body that will run its incredible course, genetically, spiritually, physically. As we move along our path on this earth, our body changes form. Think of what your body looked like and what you will look like completely naked at the age of seven, fourteen, twenty-one, thirty-five, forty-eight, fifty-nine, seventy-seven, or ninety-nine. As our life and body changes, we ascend into its new paradigm of energy and substance. All stages of our existence and all levels of our being require some form of maintenance and proper support. It is what we do with the blessing of having a physical form that is important. Who wouldn't want to keep a Ferrari at its peak performance?

You will need a few tools and tips to begin your self-healing sessions. After you read through the conditions listed below and find the issue you want to work on, you may want to gather up a few things before starting these five simple steps.

So let's get started!

1. A Spray Mist for your Chakra or Body area.
To make an essential oil mist you will need:

    a. An 8 ounce glass amber or blue glass bottle with a fine mist sprayer. You can purchase these at any health food store.
    b. A ½-ounce bottle/vial of essential oil.
    c. 7 ½ ounces of plain vodka.

Pick an essential oil listed with the condition and chakra location that resonates with your issue. Pour the essential oil into the bottle, fill the bottle to the neck with vodka, screw on the sprayer, shake vigorously, then mist above the area with 3-4 sprays.

2. Crystal, Stone Wand, or Weighted Ohm Tuning Fork.
Pick a crystal or gemstone from the list, and/or use a weighted Ohm tuning fork. When you purchase a stone, make sure it has

smooth or rounded edges. Do not use sharp edges on your body. Pick a small to medium stone or crystal wand that fits comfortably in your hand. A smooth, polished clear or rose quartz crystal can also be used for any ailment. Use your stone to gently massage the body region or chakra, or just place it over the area for 3-5 minutes.

3. **Meditation and Prayer:** You can do this on your own, or download a guided meditation to listen to. Remember, as the mind believes, the body will achieve. Visualize a brilliant crystalline light mixing with the appropriate chakra color through the region of your body needing healing. Ask God, Source, Divine, and the Angels to assist in healing this ailment and to bring healing energy to your Mind, Body, and Spirit. While you are gently massaging the region you are working on, visualize Heaven's Divine Healing Light raining down, saturating the affected area. Now visualize this brilliant crystal light mixing with the appropriate chakra color. Again, ask God, Source, Divine, and the Angels to heal this ailment and to completely spread this healing energy to your Mind, Body, and Spirit. Then:

   A. **Thank them.**
   "Dear _____, thank you for assisting me and helping me to repair my body and to thrive at my highest and best potential."

   B. **Reflect on what emotional issue you can change.**
   "Dear _____, please help me to change and put into action a change of my heart and behavior, to relieve the emotional and physical pain that is being experienced. Please empower and help me to forgive/support myself and others with love, compassion, understanding, and intention."

   C. **Visualize this issue as healed.**
   "Dear _____, thank you for removing all obstacles and blocks for this healing. Thank you for bringing clear insight, healing, and a joyous blessed life." Visualize your limb, belly, or target area, as healthy, healed, and whole. "Amen, Ohm, and So It Is."

4. **Nutrition**: We are what we eat. We all make choices that affect our body's ability to function and to nourish our souls. I have listed numerous food choices and supplements that will assist you.

5. **Movement/Exercise**: A stagnant pond of water never reaches the ocean. We have to physically "do" something to change our body and our vitality. Many people cringe at the thought of the word "exercise." But there are endless ways to move that don't entail doing reps at a gym. Thank goodness!
    a. Clean, garden, or do yard work. If you spill coffee grounds on the floor you have to physically do something to change the fact that you have a mess on your floor. You don't even think twice about grabbing a broom and cleaning it up…you just do it. Children learn from example. This is why we have so many toy kitchen sets, toddlers' popping-ball lawn mowers, and so on. If you didn't learn as a kid to move your body, that's a bummer. However, you are an adult now, so you can teach yourself.
    b. Dance. Radio is free and so is your voice. Listen to music on the radio, sing or hum a tune, then move your body to the rhythm. Don't be embarrassed, even eighteen month old babies get rave reviews for bouncing, jerking, and flailing their limbs about.
    c. Walk. Walking on two legs is a special gift, just ask any four legged creature. We do it without giving it a second thought. We can do it all day long. Walking takes us to our next destination. Walking is free. Walking clears your mind, your energy, and your spirit.
    d. Play. Playing means different things to different people. Maybe you are going to play golf, chess, hockey, or Scrabble. What you play is not important, only that you play. When you spend time doing something that makes you happy your energy and vibration rises.

Chapter 5 Chakras, Common Maladies, Simple Steps for Self-Healing

Healing with the Chakra's

Let's start with an example:

Problem: You have just signed a contract to buy a house. You are happy to be putting down roots. Your boss walks in to tell you that you have been transferred to a job across the county, and you start in three weeks.

Symptoms: You are shocked, fearful, and blown away. You feel your stomach churning, IBS starting up, and worry that you may not make it to the bathroom before your bowels let loose. Your world (root chakra) has been ripped out from underneath you.

Solution: Breathe deeply. Spritz yourself with your amazing handmade Sandalwood mist. Grab your tuning fork, strike it firmly, not your boss, and place it on your root chakra. Call on Archangels Uriel and Sandalphon to help ground you and lead you safely through this new path. Have a warm cup of dandelion tea. Get up, take a deep breath, and go home.

Light a red candle. Play *"In the Air Tonight,"* by Phil Collins, rock it, replay it, be mad, and let it out. (Excellent drumming in this tune.) Pour yourself a glass of *La Crème*, Pinot Noir, Sonoma, my favorite, sip it while roasting your potatoes and grilling your steak. Call your mom, have a good cry, tell her you love her. Eat your dinner. Go to bed. Ask God to send all of the Angels while you sleep. Tomorrow is a new day, a new beginning; your destiny is in your hands. Amen.

Read through this section and learn about what issues relate to which specific areas of the chakras. Create your plan, try it. You won't regret it!

1. The Root Chakra – Muladhara

MIND: **Color**: Red

Unbalanced Emotions: Lust, obsession, lack of security, fear of letting go, abuse, fear of moving forward, anxiousness, indecisiveness, depression,

Balanced Emotions: New beginnings, survival, vitality. prosperity, passion, purpose, success, abundance, happy family

BODY: **Location**: Base of the spine, connects us to the earth

Organ: Reproductive & adrenal glands

Stone: Ruby, red tiger's eye, bloodstone, garnet

Ailments: Addictions, constipation, hemorrhoids, colitis, crohn's, hypertension, kidney stones, sciatica, weight gain or loss, libido, glaucoma, urinary issues, diarrhea, anorexia, hip/leg/joint/knee/ankle/foot pain, anemia, varicose veins

Nourishing Foods: Red or orange foods. Carrots, potatoes, parsnips, radishes, beets, onions, garlic, eggs, meats, beans, horseradish, hot paprika, chives, cayenne pepper, edible and medicinal mushrooms, apples, cranberries, lingonberries, pomegranates, dandelion root, magnesium, and calcium citrate

SPIRIT: **Purpose**: "I am," grounding us to the earth's energy

Essential Oil: Cedarwood, sandalwood, myrrh, patchouli

Tone: Mantra chant LAM, note of C, drums

Angel: Uriel, Sandalphon

2. The Sacral Chakra – Swadhisthana

MIND: Color: Orange

Unbalanced Emotions: Fear of intimacy, hyper sexuality, unhealthy emotional attachments to others, mental or physical tension of muscles, lack of creativity, laziness

Balanced Emotions: New beginnings, survival, vitality, creativity, energy, confidence, sensual expression

BODY: Location: Two inches below the navel

Organ: Adrenals, kidneys, gonads

Stone: Carnelian, orange tourmaline, peach moonstone

Ailments: Sexual disorders, UTI's, endometriosis, fertility issues, fibroids, kidney complaints, menstrual problems, muscle cramps/spasms, issues with intestines, spleen, or gallbladder, eating disorders, emotional imbalances

Nourishing Foods: Orange/Yellow foods. Melons, mangos, strawberries, passionfruit, oranges, honey, coconut, almonds, walnuts, cinnamon, vanilla, carob, sweet paprika, sesame seeds, caraway seeds, hemp seeds, sesame seeds, wild-caught salmon, tuna, and shellfish, fennel, calendula tea, chaste tree berry, evening primrose oil

SPIRIT: Purpose: "I Feel," giving and receiving, enthusiasm, clear feeling and movement, personal power, relationships, emotions

Essential Oil: Cedarwood, sandalwood, gardenia

Tone: Mantra chant VAM, note of D, guitar

Angel: Raphael, Chamuel

3.   The Solar Plexus Chakra – Manipura

MIND: **Color**: Yellow

Unbalanced Emotions: Fear, worry, lack of courage, violence, losing your temper, despair, negativity, depression, panic attacks, anxiety, rigidity, stubbornness

Balanced Emotions: Optimism, joy, happiness, enthusiasm, positive self-esteem, a sense of freedom, peace, calmness, empowerment

BODY: **Location**: Navel to ribcage

Organ: Metabolic and digestive system, pancreas

Stone: Citrine, golden topaz, amber

Ailments: Hepatitis, food allergies, gallstones, liver issues, pancreatic problems, peptic ulcer, diabetes, kidney problems, anorexia, bulimia

Nourishing Foods: Yellow/Golden foods. Gluten-free pastas, breads, cereal, rice, seeds, sunflower seeds, goat's milk, goat and sheep cheeses, yogurt, ginger, celery, anise, peppermint, spearmint, melissa, chamomile, turmeric, cumin, fennel, yellow tomatoes and squashes, pineapple, papaya, legumes, yellow vegetables, marshmallow root or tea, monolaurin, probiotics, L-lysine, L-glutamine, cilantro, parsley, garlic, plantain, sage

SPIRIT: **Purpose**: "I Decide"

Essential Oil: Cedarwood, sandalwood, gardenia, lavender, bergamot, rosemary

Tone: Mantra chant RAM, note of E, string instruments

Angel: Michael, Uriel

Chapter 5 Chakras, Common Maladies, Simple Steps for Self-Healing

4. **The Heart Chakra - Anahata**

MIND: **Color**: Green

Unbalanced Emotions: Rejection, sadness, moodiness, mistrust, broken heart, anger, bitterness, resentment, loneliness, hate, self-centeredness, disconnection

Balanced Emotions: Tenderness, unconditional love, compassion, gratitude, acceptance, self-love, trust, loyalty, forgiveness, emotional healing, connection

BODY: **Location**: Center of chest over the sternum

Organ: Heart, lungs, thymus gland

Stone: Malachite, emerald, rose quartz, jade, peridot, chrysocolla

Ailments: Allergies, blood pressure, breast disease, circulation issues, fatigue, heart disease, immune disorders, lung issues

Nourishing Foods: Green and pink foods. Green leafy vegetables, broccoli, kale, spinach, dandelion greens, cauliflower, cabbage, celery, green tea, basil, thyme, cilantro, Coenzyme Q10, hawthorne berry, cayenne pepper, marjoram, parsley, green peppers

SPIRIT: **Purpose**: "I Love"

Essential Oil: Lavender, jasmine, rose, melissa, neroli

Tone: Mantra chant YAM, note of F, wind chimes

Angel: Raphael, Chamuel

The Throat Chakra – Vishudda

MIND: **Color**: Light blue

Unbalanced Emotions: Lying, being "wishy-washy," being overly critical, yelling, verbal abusiveness, interrupting others, rudeness, irritability, guilty feelings

Balanced Emotions: Self-expression, communication, responsibility, honesty

BODY: Location: Throat, between the collarbone and larynx

Organ: Thyroid and parathyroid

Stone: Celestine, angelite, lapis, blue opal, chrysocola, aquamarine, turquoise, blue topaz

Ailments: Asthma, bronchitis, ear infections, hearing problems, mouth ulcers, thyroid problems, tonsillitis, upper digestive tract issues, lump in throat, laryngitis, sore throat, teeth problems, thrush, jaw problems, TMJ, earaches, sinus infections, arthritis in the shoulders, sore shoulders or arms, neck problems, stress, possible drug or alcohol dependency

Nourishing Foods: Liquids in general. Water, fruit juices, herbal teas, limes, grapefruit, kiwi, apples, pears, plums, peaches, apricots, salt, lemon grass, soups, sauces, light vegetable juices, spirulina, chromium, zinc, L-tyrosine, Vitamin D3

SPIRIT: **Purpose**: "I Hear," "I Speak"

Essential Oil: Lavender, chamomile

Tones: Mantra chant HAM, note of G, singing

Angel: Gabriel

5. **The Third Eye, Brow Chakra – Ajna**

MIND: Color: Indigo

Unbalanced Emotions: Distrust, judgmental thoughts, unsympathetic, delusions, lack of empathy, lack of common sense

Balanced Emotions: Trusting your inner guidance, wisdom, insight, having a proper perspective, peace, compassion, empathy

BODY: Location: Above and between the center of the eyebrows

Organ: Pituitary gland

Stone: Lapis, purple fluorite

Ailments: Blindness, cataracts, catarrh, deafness, dyslexia, insomnia, migraine, sinus problems, visual problems, tension headache, stress, dizziness, earaches

Nourishing Foods: Dark bluish/reddish colored fruits. Blueberries, red grapes, black raspberries, red wines and grape juice, lavender, poppy seeds, mugwort, omega fatty acids, fish, nuts and seeds, eyebright, magnesium, chrysanthemum tea, raw honey, essential fatty acids, B-complex, lavender, eggplant, plums, dates, artichoke

SPIRIT: Purpose: "I See," giving and receiving, enthusiasm, clear feeling and movement, relationships, emotions, personal power

Essential Oil: Angelica, bay laurel, clary sage, cypress, frankincense, juniper, marjoram, patchouli, rosemary, sandalwood

Tone: Mantra chant AUM (Om), note of A, bells

Angel: Gabriel

6. The Crown Chakra - Sahasrara

MIND: **Color**: Violet/Gold/White

Unbalanced Emotions: Psychosis, overwhelmed, confusion, frustration, disassociation, apathy, feelings of isolation, depression, lack of inspiration, feeling ungrounded, inflexibility

Balanced Emotions: Intuitiveness, sensitive, wise, spiritually connected, aware, emotionally balanced, peaceful, calm, joyful, feelings of connectedness to heaven

BODY: **Location**: Top of the head

Organ: Pineal gland, central nervous system and brain

Stone: Amethyst, clear quartz

Ailments: Alzheimer's, depression, dizziness, epilepsy, multiple sclerosis, paralysis, Parkinson's, schizophrenia, dementia, confusion, learning difficulties, sensory problems, chronic fatigue

Nourishing Foods: White, clear, and purple foods or liquids. Coconut water, alkaline water, root, clear broth, and fasting / detoxing regimens, sage, juniper, mangosteen, DHA, monolaurin, phosphatidyl serine, gingko biloba, B-complex, CoQ10, ALA

SPIRIT: **Purpose**: "I Feel", Giving and receiving, enthusiasm, clear feeling and movement, personal power, relationships, emotions

Essential Oil: Ylang-ylang, Rosewood, Linden

Tone: Mantra chant AH, note of B, binaural brain tones, Ohm tuning forks, singing, breathing

Angel: Raphael, Chamuel

6 SPACE CLEARING – MY $25 DOLLAR LESSON

When you walk into a room, how does it feel?
Does it feel vibrant and welcoming? Does it feel empty, creepy, sad, eerie, or uncomfortable?
  I was in college and looking for a place to rent, I came across a cottage house that looked charming from the outside. It was a green one-story bungalow with massive amounts of overgrown flowers and bushes surrounding it. A small handmade sign in the front yard advertised for a roommate. I rang the doorbell, and a large, unusually odd woman answered the door. She was dressed in what I would call a muu-muu and flip-flops. I told her that I was looking for a rental and that I wanted to see the place.
  As I walked through the front door and into the living room I immediately got a sick feeling in my stomach. All the drapes were drawn, blinds were closed, and there were piles of junk and stacks of boxes everywhere. The place was organized enough to pass through the living room, dingy, but reasonably clean. The walls were pea green, and I could see the lighter-colored pea green paint behind the disheveled and poorly hung "things" on the walls.
  She led me down the hall to a tiny back bedroom. I was pleasantly surprised when she opened the door. The room had a twin bed, small dresser, a nightstand, and a lamp. The walls were a light pea green. The bed was made up with an old, creamy-colored handmade quilt. It reminded me of something from *Little House on the Prairie*. I asked what the rent was. She told me $50 dollars a month for the room and to share a bath, plus a $25 dollar deposit.

Month to month, and no lease; I could stay as long as I wanted.

I asked her who else lived there, and she pointed to the window looking out into the backyard. The backyard was also overgrown with foliage, and I saw another woman, much older than the one standing next to me, sitting in a plastic lawn chair. My inner sirens were going off and screaming at me to run. *Could this be the Bates Hotel?* I did not listen. I thought again about how nice that tiny back room appeared. I thought that for the money, it would be okay for a while, as I was as poor as a church mouse.

I asked what had happened to their former roommate and why she had moved out. The woman told me that she had had a family emergency and never actually moved her stuff in, so the room was still available. I again felt my insides getting uneasy and telling me to leave now. But how? Muu-muu was standing in the doorway to that room, filling up the space and blocking my exit. She then asked/told me to put down the deposit and just think about it for a day. She said I could come back the next day and let her know. If I did not want it, she would give me back my deposit money.

It took me a moment to respond, as I was thinking about what Hansel and Gretel had walked into. I hurriedly said okay, gave her my twenty-five dollars, and ran for my life. I felt such horrible energy in that house and from those women. When I got out to the front sidewalk I could finally breathe again. I left there knowing I would never rent that room or live in such a black hole of energy. I wanted to go back up to the door and tell her that I really didn't want to rent and to get my money back right then and there. However, I was too freaked out and afraid. I honestly felt as if I was in the presence of evil and all I wanted to do was flee.

Somehow I found the courage to go back the next day to let them know that I would not be renting, and to get my $25 dollars back. As I walked up to the house I got that sick creepy feeling in my body again. I knew I had made the right decision.

I rang the bell and knocked on the front door. I could see them through the window. I was glad they were home. To my surprise I watched them get up and go to the back of the house. I went around to the back door and knocked again. Maybe they didn't see me? I then watched them through the back door window, going back to the front of the house. I ran around to the front of the house and rang the front doorbell again. This time they just stood on the other side of the front door, looking at me through the window and laughing. They were never going to give me my deposit money back. I had been scammed by two dark, *creepy* horrible human beings. I wondered how many other poor college students had been innocently lured into their snare. I don't think they ever had a roommate or had any intention of renting that back room to anyone. They were just bottom feeders, looking to steal from others.

I did not listen to my gut. I did not listen to the screaming coming from inside my body telling me to run. I did not listen to my intuition the moment I walked into that house. I "knew" the moment I stepped inside, that something was really off energetically, and so were those people. Had I listened to my soul, to my intuition, I would not have had such a costly and unpleasant lesson.

The time we spend in our own space affects us more than we think. No one really wants to hang out in a funeral home just for fun because it has great vibes. No one spends their afternoon picnicking and soaking up all the "good energy" at the local garbage dump. Spaces have energy, just like people do.

When our space, home, or office does not feel "right," we actually do have the power and ability to change it. Space clearing has been used for as long as human beings have been on Earth. Every culture has their own way to clear the energy and raise the vibration of their own space. I have found that I like a blend of these many techniques. You will find that you like specific techniques as well.

The steps:
1. The Feeling
   How does the house, room, area feel? Dark, stagnant, creepy, scary, unsettled, or chaotic? Pick a word that describes the feeling, as this is what you want to clear and hold in your intention.
2. The Intention
   What feeling or energy do you want to have in this area? Happy, joyful, creative, calming, energetic, alive, or welcoming? Pick a word that describes what you need to feel in this area.
3. The Tools
   a. Sage, smudge stick, nonflammable container--ashtray, pot, or dish.

You can use some sage spice from a jar in your kitchen, or you can purchase a sage smudge stick. Place a small amount of sage in a nonflammable container. Use a lighter or matches to light it, blow it out, and "smoke" the area you are clearing. Don't forget to open a few windows and doors. A smoke alarm going off in the middle of a clearing is a bit distracting! If you use a smudge stick, light it, blow it out, and wave the smudge stick in the air and around through the areas you are clearing. Make sure not to drop the embers and set something on fire. Many people think using an abalone shell for a container is spiritual, cool, or fancy. I agree that it looks cool, but they have holes in them, get really hot, will scorch, and you can burn your hand or drop embers on the floor. Always flush the ashes down the toilet when you are done. Ashes to ashes, dust to dust. Ask Mother Earth to recycle the ash--just as she does after a forest fire. From the ashes begets a new and beautiful forest, just like your space.

  b. Sweetgrass braid

Sweetgrass is used after you finish your clearing. You can purchase sweetgrass from a local store or pick some, dry it, and braid your own. Light the sweetgrass braid, blow it out, and walk through your space again, blowing or fanning the smoke into the areas. Say a prayer of thanks to heaven for assisting you in blessing your space. Flush the ashes.

  c. Salt or salt water

You can sprinkle salt in corners, or mist the area with a sprayer of salt and water mixed. Salt cleanses energy. If you want to clear the energy from old jewelry, simply place the jewelry in a bowl and pour dry salt over it. Leave it there for a few days. Wash it off, say your prayer, and put it back on.

  d. Crystals

Clear quartz, rose quartz, black tourmaline, citrine, lapis, coral, malachite, ruby, or other crystals. Pick one to absorb the negative energy and pick one to infuse the area with positive energy. I use a black tourmaline to absorb the heavy feeling. I use any other crystal to add back the good energy, depending on how I feel about the situation. The choice of the crystal does not really matter. It is your intention that matters most. Be sure to thank both crystals for their help in your endeavor. I set crystals in the sun for 24 hours to reenergize when I am finished.

e. Holy water

You do not have to buy sacred or holy water from a business. Simply place clean spring water in your container and pray over or bless it. I personally ask God, Divine, Source, all the Angels in heaven, my guides, and crossed-over loved ones to bless the water. "May everything that it touches be graced with love, light, and healing, Amen." I use a clear glass bottle with a fine mist sprayer. I use bottled spring water or PH water. I make a label for the bottle that says: Holy water, love, joy, peace, abundance, light, healing, or another positive term. Much research has been done on the properties of water molecules from bottles that have positive words on them and from bottles that have negative words. It is fascinating to see the difference in the molecules under a microscope. Google this topic; you won't be sorry. Got to love science! I also sometimes pour the water over a favorite crystal as it funnels into the glass sprayer. You can use almost anything to help you set your intention and infuse your holy water with God's Light.

f. Candles

I like to use a 7-day prayer candle. I usually pick a white candle. You can also use a small votive candle that burns out within the hour. Make sure you place it safely so you don't burn your house down! The moment I strike the match I start my prayer for love, light, and healing. When I light the wick of the candle, I set my final intention. I ask all of heaven to come and restore new life-force energy to the area. I tell all chaotic energy to leave and to transmutate back to a higher vibration.

g. Essential oil spray
I like to make my own essential oil spray. The recipe for making a spray is explained previously in this chapter. I lightly mist the entrance to each passageway, doorway, or door. My favorite essential oil is Rose Absolute. Lavender, myrrh, rosemary, geranium, eucalyptus, neroli, cedarwood, grapefruit, and many others make a nice spray. Pick the one that resonates with your soul. It matters not what others may think or tell you, as this is your space, not theirs.

h. Tuning fork
I like to use many different tuning forks, depending on what I feel. I suggest starting with an unweighted Ohm tuning fork. I strike the tuning fork on a hockey puck to get the vibration started. I spiral it around myself first, clearing my energy, and then walk around the room spiraling the tuning fork up and out. I know when I am done, because I feel it. You will feel when you are done also. Striking it one to three times is usually enough for an average size room.

i. Bells, chimes, singing bowls, drums
Bells are easy to carry around. You can ring them in tight areas, corners, over furniture, or in locations that have heavy energy. A few rings with good intentions will clear the energy. Small chimes work nicely, but some can be too large for easy usage and must be struck with a mallet. Singing bowls are amazing, but very cumbersome to carry around. Hand-held drums are also great for clearings.

j. Pendulum
A pendulum comes in handy when you first walk into a room to check for heavy energy. I like to use a small crystal pendulum, about the size of a marble. They are usually sold with a metal chain on them. I replace the chain with embroidery thread. I tie a few large double knots at the top. I only use about 8 inches of finished thread length. I wet the cotton threading or string. Water conducts electricity very nicely, and I have found

that I can physically feel the energy in my fingers and hand when I use a wet string on my pendulum. Holding the pendulum still, I slowly move it through the area I am checking. You will feel it dragging or pulling through the air. The air will feel foggy or thick. This is a very unusual sensation for most people to experience. There is nothing to fear. Some people describe feeling as if the hair is standing up on the back of their neck. Our body teaches us to be afraid when this happens to us. It can be a signal to avoid lightning or the feeling we get meeting a person who has "bad" energy. This is merely your body's antennae giving you information about an area you need to clear with a bell, chime, gong, clapping, or other method.

k. Statue, object, or photo

I like to bring a small statue of my angel of the day when I do a clearing. I usually pick Archangel Michael. He is great at cutting etheric cords that bind us to another's energy. For me, his statue is a nice reminder that I have him watching my back and helping me to clear the space. Sometimes I bring my other carved stone angels with me for the day. Use your gut intuition, feelings, and invite that angel to help you. Photos are another nice thing to have with you when you clear your space. Pick a photo of a joyful, happy time. Pick something that reminds you of the feeling you are trying to add to your space.

l. Feathers

I use a small set of feathers made into angel wings. They are easy to hold, create a nice breeze, and move the air where I have misted with essential oil spray. A simple large feather will do the same. Make sure to set your intention that the feather will clear the energy, sending it to heaven and replacing the energy with love, joy, happiness, peace, or other positive vibration.

m. Cocoa nibs

Don't forget the outside area of your space. Cocoa nibs are raw chopped cocoa beans. You can buy them at any grocery store. Bless your plants, trees, birds, and wild animals for being part of your life. Bless the elemental angels and fae for watching over your home. Toss raw cocoa nibs into the yard, sprinkling them into the corners, along the fence line, and so on. People love natural settings like botanical gardens, beautiful lawns, lakes, ponds, forests, and trails. Why? Because these environments ground our souls and make us feel good. We need to refresh, clear, and bless what makes us feel at one with heaven. Have you ever told your children to go outside and play because it's good for them? Have you ever said you need to take a walk to clear your mind? You get my point.

n. North, South, East, West, Above, Below, and your actual earthly space. Energy is all around us. You want to set your intention to clear all directions of your space and make it inviting to all that enter and to all who live there. Your physical energy extends beyond your body. When you get close to someone and they are hot, cold, angry, or happy, you know it, because you can "feel" their energy before you touch them. Try closing your eyes, reach out to someone, and stop before you actually touch them. Feel their energy. You will be able to do it with a little practice. The same is true for your living space. Its energy extends beyond its physical location. Have you ever walked up to a person's front door or a business's entrance, hesitated, changed your mind, and walked away? Why? It probably didn't feel good, inviting, or pleasant to you. You trusted your intuition and avoided the bad energy. This is what space clearing is all about. Feeling your space's energy, clearing the chaotic heavy energy, and replacing it with heaven's love and light.

o. Your Hands and your Heart
If you don't have the time or money to acquire various tools or "equipment" to do your own space clearing, that is not a problem. All you need are your hands and intention. You really only need to do three things. Clap your hands together a few times as you are raising them up in the air. Flick your fingers toward the sky,

and tell the energy to leave. Spiral your hands above your head and then down to your feet as you ask heaven to bring love and light into your space. Say your prayer of thanks. Envision your space with sparkly beautiful light. Say Amen, and So It Is, or whatever you say to close your conversation with heaven.

I have a routine that I have settled on for space or energy clearing over the years. It may or may not feel right for you, but it is a start. You can incorporate any or all parts of it. Just follow your heart.

1. When I get to the door, I pay attention to how I am feeling, and ask what is the feeling of this space?
2. I place a small white cloth on a table in the heart or gathering area of the house.
3. I set out my things--crystals, candles, etc.--on the white cloth.
4. I say my prayer of intention and ask that God and the Angels be with me. I light the candle.
5. I walk through the house and use a pendulum to feel where it drags.
6. I use sage smudging and start at the front door.
7. I carry my bells, chimes, essential oil sprays, tuning forks, angel feathers, etc., in my carpenter's belt. Yup, my husband bought me a carpenter's belt twenty years ago to wear when I am creating a new painting. Little did he know that I would eventually turn it into an energy clearing accessory!
8. As I move through each area I instinctively use my "accessories" to clear and repair the energy. Do you or should you use essential oil spray, holy water misting, chimes, a tuning fork, or salt water spray? This is where you have to trust your gut and act accordingly. Your feelings are not wrong, and you will know or feel what it is you need to do.
9. When I have completed the inside space I move to the outside area and repeat the process.
10. Once I am satisfied with how things are feeling, I go back to the front door and use the sweetgrass smoke. I go back through the house and outside area, fanning the sweetgrass smoke with my feather angel wings.

11. I say a final blessing and ask for clearing and renewing to the north, south, east, west, above, below, and current location. I thank heaven and ask for a blessing for the people and souls who reside there. I ask that only heaven's light and energy fill that space, Amen.

These are my basic guidelines for space clearing. This will help you get started doing your own blessings. You don't have to do all of the steps every time. If you have just received a prank phone call, a simple thought with focused intention to clear that energy, and a spritz of essential oil spray should get the job done!

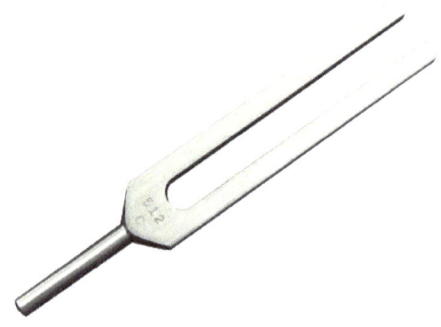

7 MEDITATION & PRAYER

Meditation and prayer are simply heavenly conversations in our minds. I have said my prayers for as long as I can remember. How does a child learn to pray, and to whom without any formal training? I believe we are born with this ability, this knowing. My prayers as a child started out pretty basic and mostly involved praying for injured animals I found and the many sad situations I encountered. I also prayed that I would be good enough--but for what? I would say my prayers over and over until I could finally fall asleep. When I woke I always remembered exactly where I left off and continued until I finished them the next morning. I would then move on to my morning prayers.

I was not into wasting time so I didn't tuck into a kneeling position at the end of my bed. I always did my praying in my head, just me and my conversations with heaven. I have never prayed out loud and I still don't. When in church people are expected to "repeat after me" or sing out loud. For many people this is comforting. For me this is impossible and quite terrifying. I have experienced the looks from people who are judging me while my mouth is silent in church. They don't know what my conversation is with God. They don't know that even as a child, just walking into a holy space brought me to tears and rendered me speechless.

I went with my best friend in high school to her church on many occasions. Once, on Ash Wednesday, I went across the street with SHL to be blessed with her and have "ashes" placed on my forehead, just like all of the other classmates whose families went to this small-town church. She told me not to say anything and everything would be fine. Just do what she did. The priest greeted SHL and said hello to me. I opened my mouth and said I had never done this before, then asked what I was supposed to say or do. The priest took me out of the line and told me I had to sit in the back of the church, that he could not bless me and that I did not belong there.

I did go sit in the back pew of that church. Then I got up and quietly left before anyone noticed. I felt so worthless and ashamed. I was apparently not good enough to be part of their private prayer group. I wondered how the mean kids in that line could be welcomed and blessed, and not me. I wondered why the lunch money that I earned at my job and put in their offering basket was good enough to keep, yet I was not welcome on this "holy" day. This is another reason I find it hard to speak in a place of worship. I worship daily from my heart and in my mind, body, and soul.

I can always be found driving in my car talking to God, asking for heaven's Angelic assistance, saying "Hi" to my DPs (my dead people), asking my Guides to help me be the best I can be. I always ask God to use me as a vessel of Love, Light, and Healing for others and to raise my vibration, abilities, and gifts to a higher level. When I change the channel on the radio, I usually get a song with a title or words exactly the same as I was just sharing with heaven. That always makes me smile-- confirmation that my message was sent and received. I know that I have probably had more conversational words with heaven than with actual people…though my husband may disagree.

Being told that you have to properly meditate is always a challenge. Especially when people are telling you to clear your mind, hold still, don't fall asleep; don't look them in the eye, and so on. I have realized that steps and instruction are helpful, but why do some people say you have to do it their way or it won't work? Meditation and mindfulness are just those…*thoughts you have in your mind*, conversations with Source, God, and yourself. That is what it's all about.

We all have thoughts all of the time. It is what we focus our thoughts on that matters, thoughts become reality. As your skill set and focus grows you will find exactly what works for you. You will be drawn to learn from others with whom you resonate. You only need three things for prayer or meditation: a topic, a request, and a thank you. Let's get started:

1. When you are driving down the road, vacuuming your house, washing dishes, taking out the trash, what are you thinking about? We are all thinking about small things, big things, and sometimes nothing. This is a perfect time to reflect on one particular thought, and simply ask for guidance and a sign or epiphany to come to you. It is very easy to attach a sticky note to your trash can with a message about what you need help with. Every time you take out the trash you will be thinking about this "issue" and asking for assistance and guidance. Repetition becomes habit. Thinking about something is meditation. If I say "cat," you see a cat in your head. It makes no difference if the cat is a tabby or a panther; it is your cat. When I walk into a holy space I see, and feel in my body, the Christ light, and every time my mind goes to prayer and meditation. If I bang my elbow and it is killing me, I envision the energy and light from God/Source running through my elbow and healing my cells. I then run the energy through the earth and back to heaven. This takes me only a few moments. This is meditation, healing meditation, and it doesn't have to last for an hour. How many times have you heard, "Let me meditate

Chapter 7 Meditation & Prayer

on it and I'll get back to you".... "Let me think about it" ...this is the same thing. If the person gets back to you right away from thinking or meditating on the issue, do you discount it unless they make you wait twenty minutes, two hours, two weeks, or two months? No, you respect the fact that they even took the time to consider your request. Meditation is thinking and reflecting in your own mind, in a peaceful manner. Music, no music, doesn't matter. Meditation does not mean you have to sit like a pretzel and have a blank mind. I always have a goal when I think about something or meditate.

Do you normally get into your car and drive around not having any idea of where you want to go? Probably not!

    a.   Mapping out in your mind where you want to go or what you want to achieve is really not that hard. If I say New York, you see New York in your head. If you want to go to New York, then visualize yourself getting on a plane and landing in New York. Visualize yourself doing the things you want to do when you are there. This feels very much like making a grocery list in your mind.

    b.   Imagine a ray or beam of light from the sky/heaven/God/Source passing right through you into the earth, as you think, contemplate, meditate on your thought, idea, or question.

    c.   If you have an injury or sore body part, imagine the light passing directly through this area with brighter light. Now imagine your cells healing and changing from dark or painful to light and no pain. Imagine yourself and your body part as healthy and functioning perfectly.

    d.   If you can only do this for 15 or 30 seconds, that is great. Every time you visualize the light moving through you, you are accomplishing your goal. Soon you will find that the time you spend on this healing will increase naturally. Practice makes perfect, just like learning to play an instrument, or like driving home from a new destination. Eventually it becomes autopilot.

e. When to stop self-healing or meditating on a goal? When the issue resolves to your satisfaction. You will instinctively know when you are done and how often you should "meditate." It will become as natural to you as knowing how much water you want to drink or when you want to go to sleep.

These are photographic examples of healing energy after a little meditation with focused intention. I ask for them to be by my side and to help me. I feel them arrive, I see them, and I take a picture.

8 COINCIDENCE, SERENDIPITY, NUDGES, SMACKDOWNS, & FATE

Coincidence: is a remarkable concurrence of events or circumstances that have no apparent connection with each other.
Serendipity: means a "fortunate happenstance" or "pleasant surprise."
Nudge: to prod (someone) gently in order to draw their attention to something.
Smackdowns: Humbling experiences that happen when we are cocky and not paying attention.
Fate: Something we have no control over.

Have you ever had a weird random mental thought about something and then said to yourself that you should check it out? Maybe the next day you overhear a stranger talking on their phone to someone about the same thing you had just thought about. You are on your way home, and the bus that drives by happens to have that "thought," "thing," or "idea," splashed across the side of it. There's your sign. It's as simple and clear as "Larry the Cable Guy."

Coincidence

Coincidence happens randomly and is a surprising experience. Coincidence, in my opinion, is two concurring events that will eventually intersect. Let's say two people are going to college to study tabby cats. These two people are in two different classrooms with two different professors, but end up at the bookstore grabbing the same book about tabby cats. Coincidence? Let's move forward twenty years. These two students are now PhD's and both are in Sweden to observe these tabby cats. They run into each other at another bookstore grabbing for the same book. Is this coincidence?

I believe that many people are here for the same learning lesson and that we will eventually run into them again. It does not mean that we are supposed to be with that person. It means that we are not alone. It means that there are kindred spirits with the same interests. It is an opportunity to connect and share what we have learned, and to learn something new from someone else. Coincidence is an opportunity to connect and to grow.

Serendipity

Serendipity happens when we ask for divine intervention. Heaven will not intervene on our behalf without our permission or our asking. Assume you ask Archangel Raphael to help you while you run your errands. You have very little time to get a million things done, and you don't know how you can humanly accomplish this. You are driving your car in bumper-to-bumper traffic, worrying about being late. You ask Archangel Raphael to clear a path for you if it is in your highest and best good. Suddenly a police car shows up to divert the traffic. You are the first car he motions out of traffic to drive up the side of the highway. Nice job, Raphael. You then get to your appointment and there is no place to park. You ask Raphael to find you a "snackbar parking" space. Bazinga…the car parked by the front door starts to back out and the driver motions you to park there. Your entire day of appointments and chores has become a smooth and joyous event. When we ask for assistance, heaven is waiting to jump in, if it is in our highest and best good.

Personal serendipitous events are a fun thing for me to share and reflect on. One day in Stockholm, Sweden, we were with our daughters, enjoying the sites and the history of the country. We ate reindeer steaks, lots of frozen butter with rock salt sprinkled on the top, drank lingonberry booze in an ice cup at the Ice Bar while freezing our butts off, and generally had a very interesting time. I had been saying my prayers and talking to heaven while we explored the city. I asked for divine intervention to lead us to something really unique and unexpected. I also asked for a sign as to whether I should buy a rug, either of reindeer or a wolf-hide. I am not into killing helpless animals for their fur. I am into respecting, honoring, and using all parts of an animal when its life has ended humanely.

We were walking by an interesting shop not too far from the King's palace when I noticed a unique lamp in the window. This was a store for children, with many pretty items of clothing and stuffed furry toys in the window. But that lamp, oh my. This lamp had a hand-embroidered lampshade, an antler as the stem, and a hand-carved wooden base. On top of the wooden base was a kitten. A taxidermied kitten. The antler stem of the lamp went right through the sleeping kitten's body. Holy crap! I had never seen anything like it! As macabre as this lamp may have been to others, it was really beautiful to me. I went into the shop by myself. My husband and daughters thought I had lost my mind. I talked to the shop owner and found out that her husband was a taxidermist and that the kitten had been theirs and had died. I wanted to buy the lamp right then and there, but my husband said no way. He was grossed out by that poor kitten. We had always joked that we would turn our dog Portnoy into a hassock after he passed away because he was so soft. Sick humor, I know, but true.

So, I had my sign. No kitten lamp, no reindeer rug, no wolf rug. Thanks to the intervention of heaven, I got my answer: "No."

Nudges

Nudges happen when you have asked for intervention, but are not paying attention to the clues or signs you asked for. Nudges can be good. We were finishing our walk around Stockholm and came upon a brewery bar. We went inside to warm up and drink a Swedish beer. On our table was a flyer for a maritime museum named Vasa. I put the flyer in my pocket and didn't think about it again. The next day we were strolling around Stockholm and a bus passed by with a picture of a ship named *Vasa*. We stopped for an ice cream cone in the park, and yes, you can buy ice cream cones outside in February in Sweden. I overheard some people in line talking about the *Vasa*. I reached into my winter coat pocket and pulled out the brochure. I decided this would be our next adventure. We jumped on a bus and went to the museum, much to my family's chagrin.

I had goosebumps as we walked up to the entrance, and it wasn't from the cold air. My scalp was tingling and I felt as if I had been there before. As we started touring the museum I stopped to read a plaque on the wall. I dang near fainted. The *Vasa's* maiden voyage was on August 10, 1628. My birthday is August 10th. The poor ship sailed only 1,300 meters, keeled over, and sank to the bottom. The *Vasa* stayed underwater for 333 years. She was brought to the surface for the first time on April 24, 1961. She went down on my birthday, and rose again during my first year of life. Crazy stuff you can't make up. What really struck me was that I had done a painting of a ship that looked exactly like the *Vasa* when I was a freshman in high school. I completed that ship painting on my birthday, signed my name to the canvas, and felt my usual relief and satisfaction. I honestly wondered if I had been on the *Vasa* a few hundred years ago.

This is an example of a good nudge. Nudges are painless. I would have never known about the *Vasa* without a few nudges and then following my gut.

Smack Downs

Smackdowns are just that; you get smacked down. Smackdowns happen when we don't pay attention to friendly nudges. I don't personally like smackdowns. I feel like a complete moron or flying chimp when it happens to me. Smackdowns happen to all of us from time to time. But they don't happen if we pay attention and if we come from a place of love.

A sad little story from my childhood, and yes, smackdowns can happen to children:

In the late fall of fourth grade I decided to climb down a sinking silo in the back field--not a smart idea, since we had lost a cow in a sinkhole next to that hundred-year-old silo. But, I was very curious about what was at the bottom of that silo. I carefully climbed downward on the rusted ladder that was still hanging by a thread. When I reached the bottom of the silo it smelled sticky sweet, much like old hay and molasses. However, it was simply rotten and decaying silage....what a concept!

The ground was very soft, and it was rather warm down there. I noticed movement on the ground from the corner of my eye. I followed the movement and saw a smooth black shiny tail sticking out of a pile of silage. I walked over very gently and thrust my hand out to grab the tail. Out *popped* a nice-size black salamander with yellow spots! I had a new friend. I petted my salamander a few times and then put him in my pocket while I pondered about how to raise him. I climbed back up and out of that old silo. I skipped to the cow barn to find a cardboard box. After I picked the perfect box, I started designing my friend's new digs. I made a staircase, curtains, a bed for him out of an old cereal box, used Saran Wrap for windows, and tissues for carpet. I put a cup of water and some grass in "Sam's" new pad. I then wrapped the entire cardboard box in Saran Wrap, poked a few holes in the top for air, and felt super happy. I decided that Sam would be lonely if he didn't have a roommate. I cut some fabric out of a shirt of mine in the shape of a salamander. I hand-sewed it together and filled it with dried beans. Perfect, a roommate for my friend. I never wanted anyone to be lonely.

I took "Sam" to school with me the next day. Ms. "Teacher" was shocked, but told me that I could keep "Sam" in the aquarium with Richard's turtle. Richard's family owned a bank. They had bought an aquarium for our class so his turtle could be with him at school. Sam was going to have a live roommate! Sam lived at school in that aquarium for a few months. He ate the turtle's food items (bugs, flies, worms) and seemed to be thriving nicely. I held him every day. I talked to him every day. I was a good mom.

Christmas break was coming, and the teacher said we had to take our pet's home. I told her that I couldn't take him home and that they didn't even know I had a salamander as a pet. She said he could stay for the holiday break as long as he had enough food. Great! At the end of the school day, when the turtle was boxed up, I dumped the little remaining "yucky bug food" into the aquarium and bid Sam goodbye for the break. He had food, he was small, and I figured that he didn't eat much. He would be just peachy until I returned.

After Christmas break all of the kids came back in January showing off what they'd gotten for Christmas. That was cool and fun to see all their neat presents. I had nothing I wanted to share so I immediately went to the aquarium to spend time with Sam. He looked a little dry and a tad skinny. He wasn't wiggling around like he used to. I reached into the tank to grab him. As my fingers got close to his head he clamped onto my pointer finger. I darn near had a heart attack. I screamed and flung my hand out of the tank, with Sam still on my finger. Sam went flying into the stratosphere; hit the

Chapter 8 Coincidence, Serendipity, Nudges, Smackdowns, & Fate

brick schoolroom wall, then went "splat" on the painted concrete floor. I had just killed Sam. I starved him and then I catapulted him to a sudden death. I cried while the other kids laughed. Bad morning for the first day back from Christmas break. Very very bad day for Sam.

Lunchtime came and it was a bright sunny day, but the playground was covered in snow and had a few muddy wet spots. The teacher told me to stay inside and read since I didn't have proper clothing or boots to go outside. I ignored her and headed for the door. All the girls went running out to the swings. They had snow boots; I did not. I walked carefully, jumped, and hopped to reach the swings without ruining my shoes and my new white knee-high Christmas socks. I was so proud of the socks I got for Christmas. They were pretty, super fluffy, and soft.

One of the girls in the group was always nice to me. Her father would pick her up after school in his big brown truck. He would also give her a candy bar when he picked her up. Sometimes he would give her a 7-UP bar. This old-time candy bar could be broken into seven pieces of candy, much like a Whitman's chocolate assortment. When she got this particular candy bar she would break off one end, get out of the truck, and give me a piece. She would then hop back in her dad's truck and they would drive away. I was quite the lone wolf as a child, so her kindness and sharing confused me, but made me feel happy.

Back to the playground. This generous and kind girl was swinging and playing with the rest of the girls in our class. Her mother had filled her coat pockets with peppermint candy to share that day. She gave everyone a peppermint candy. I bit mine in half and put the rest in my pocket for later. There was a particularly mean girl in that class. We all remember one, don't we? Mean Girl's family owned several businesses, so she was a privileged kid. She was like Veruca Salt in *Willy Wonka and the Chocolate Factory*. Just plain mean. This mean chubby-bully asked me what I got for Christmas. I told her I got socks. She made fun of me and said I was lying. She came over to me and pushed me down. She pulled my shoes off and threw them onto the snow bank. She then grabbed my arm, pulled me to my feet, and dragged me through the mud without my shoes. My socks were ruined, and I felt humiliated. The generous girl who shared her candy bars collected my shoes and brought them to me. I was so distraught and angry that instead of thanking her for helping me, I did something really stupid. I still had that small piece of chewed-up peppermint in my mouth. I told her I had a secret I wanted to share. When she leaned in to hear my secret, I spit my candy in her ear. The second I did that horrible thing to her, I realized that I had made a huge mistake. I had lashed out at the person who was trying to help me. She ran crying back inside the school.

It was time to meet my maker. I marched myself back into school and stood in front of my teacher. My smack down was about to begin.

My smackdown:

1. I had to write a million words about how to care for salamanders and what I did wrong, and read it to the class.
2. I had mud-colored socks.
3. I had zero self-esteem left.
4. I got no more candy from the nice girl, and I couldn't blame her for avoiding me.
5. I remained a lone wolf for the rest of the year, reading my books during recess and the lunch break.

Chapter 8 Coincidence, Serendipity, Nudges, Smackdowns, & Fate

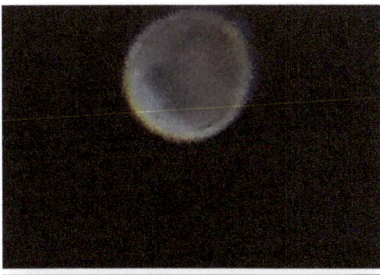

In my child's mind, this smackdown was well deserved. I had starved, murdered, destroyed, and assaulted, all in the same day. Why didn't I listen to the advice and "nudges" I had been given? I have never forgotten that day and how it changed me, for the good. I shared this story with my husband over a glass of wine while I was writing this section. He laughed and thought it was a great story to share. It took me a few days to consider his "nudge' for me to share from the heart. Since I have no desire to have another smackdown, you got the story.

FATE

The definition of fate is the development of events *beyond* a person's control, regarded as, determined by, a supernatural power.

I hear people tell me that a particular "thing" was "fate" and that they had no control over their behavior in "that" situation. Really?

Fate is only one thing to me. We get a round-trip ticket to Earth, we are born, and we die, simple and true. Everything else, well, we have choice, intention, and free will.

If I decide to build my house on an active volcano, is it fate that destroyed my house? Or was it stupidity and choice?

Destiny is not Fate. Destiny is following your path, with love and kindness leading the way. Fate is being born and going back home again to Heaven.

We have the power to change our lives and other's lives for the good. We also have the choice as to whether we blatantly ignore, inflict pain, create drama and chaos, or deliberately refuse to help others. Turning a blind eye does not improve our quality of Mind, Body, and Spirit.

Let's say you are at a crosswalk signal, and there is an old grandma with a walker who you can see won't be able to cross by herself. You are in a hurry; the light changes and you bolt. She struggles to cross and gets hit by a car. Was her death fate? No. It was your unwillingness to intervene, lead with love, and do unto others. What is your smackdown? Trying to sleep at night after reading in the paper that the grandmother you ignored was raising her two grandchildren, because her son and daughter-in-law died, and now those kids are completely alone. The smackdown is living with the guilt of what you didn't do and could have--should have--prevented. That is a tough pill to swallow.

Chapter 8 Coincidence, Serendipity, Nudges, Smackdowns, & Fate

Chapter 9 Putting It All Together

9 PUTTING IT ALL TOGETHER

We are all born with intuitive and innate survival skills. Little children instinctively cry when they "feel" they have done something wrong. If a puppy is just lying there we ask ourselves what is wrong. Of course animals can't speak human words; they show us by their expression. Somehow we instinctively and intuitively know that we need to take them to the vet. Are these just observations, or are we communicating without words? If we are communicating without words, is it our telepathy and psychic abilities coming forth? Yes.

The best medicine, in my opinion, is a balance of Mind, Body, and Spirit. We have the opportunity in this lifetime to keep this "trinity" healthy and in balance. We have the ability to repair, enrich, heal, grow, and enhance our wellbeing in all aspects of our lives.

This book was written to share what I have learned and to encourage you to explore and learn more about the incredible gifts we were born with and about the tools we were given to do so.

Our world, our lives, our souls are three-dimensional. Just because you can't physically see behind a building doesn't mean that nothing exists behind that building.

Putting it all together can seem daunting. So let's take an example:

Chanel is a healthy, happy, and busy lady. Chanel does everything for everyone else. She becomes tired, cranky, and feels unappreciated because she is so busy. She doesn't say her prayers in the car on the way to work anymore; she drinks espresso and screams

Chapter 9 Putting It All Together

at people on her cell phone. She parks her car, gets out, and dumps her purse all over the ground. Her hormones are changing these days and she gets snarky with everyone. She is bored at her job. She ignores the horrible sound in her car engine because she is overwhelmed. Her car dies on the highway in a snowstorm. She spends four hours in a blizzard freezing her butt off, waiting for a tow truck. She wakes up the next day feeling like she has the flu. She goes to work anyway. Her co-workers get sick, they all leave work, and a contract deadline is missed. She quietly gets blamed for the business's financial problems. Chanel now really hates herself and her job.

She finally goes to her doctor and is told that her bloodwork is great and nothing is wrong with her, except that she has Chronic Fatigue Syndrome. She is given an antidepressant and sent home.

Chanel quits her job because she has a diagnosis and believes she will be sick for the rest of her life. She is angry with heaven and wants to know what she did to deserve this punishment. She withdraws from her family and friends. Her husband leaves her and the kids run wild….you get the picture.

How could this story have gone?

Chanel is a healthy, happy, and busy lady. Chanel helps others and takes time for herself. She drives to work saying prayers of gratitude, lets other drivers into traffic, and when she parks her car, she finds a shiny dime on the ground. "Pennies from Heaven," and she smiles. She feels great after her yoga class so she cooks dinner for her family and brings a plate of food to the neighbor with a broken leg. Her hormones are changing these days and she notices that she gets snarky with everyone. She decides to trust her intuition, listen to her inner voice, and starts taking Chaste tree berry, evening primrose oil, a B-complex, 5-HTP, and some minerals. She now feels great and more inspired to bring new and creative ideas to her work. She hears a horrible sound in her car engine so she immediately stops at a car repair shop. She asks Archangel Michael to keep her safe and Archangel Raphael to help her on her travels, she then says Thank you, and Amen. Her car is easily fixed and she is safe to drive home in a snowstorm. While she is driving home in that blizzard she stops to give another soul a lift, as their car had broken down.

She wakes up the next day feeling great. She goes to work to find that the person she helped last night has left her a fruit bowl and a meat and cheese basket with a thank-you card. Her co-workers think is she great, so they agree to eat the lunch basket instead of leaving early, so they can all work together to beat the business deadline and get a bonus. She gets the credit for leading by example, helping others in need, supplying lunch, and gets an additional bonus from her boss. Chanel is proud of her health, proud of her behavior, and proud of taking care of herself, which allowed her to take good care of others.

She goes to her doctor and is told that her bloodwork is great and nothing is wrong, she has a clean bill of health. She tells her doctor that she meditates, does yoga, prays, takes supplements, and eats a clean diet. She is told to keep up the good work and "see you next year."

Chanel gets a promotion. Her husband brags about her to his friends. They can afford that European vacation and art classes for their kids. She lives her blessed life happily ever after ....you get the picture, she followed her gut, her intuition.

We don't have to tackle everything at once. Trying to improve all areas of our Mind, Body, and Spirit all at once can be daunting and close to impossible. All we have to do is to pick one thing at a time and change it.

Maybe this week we change from drinking soda pop to drinking green tea. We read a book on alternative healing. We take simple steps we can stick with to change our lives.

I have known too many people who have had a viral sore throat and do nothing about it, only to let it turn into a huge health mess. All they had to do was to take some zinc lozenges and use a neti pot or gargle with saltwater. It would have speeded up their healing. So simple. So easy. If you can't do that for whatever reason, why not ask your Angels to help you heal. Just try "something." The point is that we have to change our thinking and behavior to change our outcome.

Putting it all together happens in stages. This book is meant to enlighten, educate, and open your mind to other possibilities regarding Mind, Body, and Spirit. If there is a chapter that interests you, learn more about it. Go to the library or bookstore and educate yourself on the topic you are drawn to. What I have found is that for my entire life, the more I learn, the more I realize what I don't know. That drives me to learn more. Our brain and soul have an unlimited potential to grow and expand, if we chose so. The more I ask to feel, hear, see, and connect to Spirit, Heaven, Divine, God, and the Angels, the more I'm shown.

Heaven truly enjoys educating us, communicating with us, and helping us on our healing path. The more we evolve and learn here, the better we care for ourselves and others, the more we lead with love, the better it is for us--really great when we finish our lessons here on Earth and then return home. All we have to do is ask, be open to receive, and believe in something greater than ourselves.

Past History-Herstory

Our past tells us much about who we are, based on what we have experienced. Regardless of whether we are a man or a woman. Our past allows us to pick and choose which parts we don't want to repeat and which parts we can use to help us change our choices for our future. Our present is a simply a report card on how we are doing so far. Our future is our choice, of our free will, our intention; and only we determine the outcome.

Over the years I have heard so many times that someone keeps doing a "bad" thing or exhibiting destructive behavior because that was the way they were raised. It is not their fault they are the way they are. Really?

If as a child you were neglected or abused, does that mean it is perfectly fine to do the same to your child? Adults get to make choices, children are not so lucky.

If you were poor and had an outhouse, like me, does that mean you should stay poor and have an outhouse too? If your parents didn't get to go to school, does that mean that you shouldn't go to school?

Pick almost any subject, topic, or item (short of a bag full of priceless diamonds) and see what you think of this comment that I have heard way too many times: "If it was good enough for me, it should be good enough for you!" That saying makes my soul sick, I completely disagree.

Wishing someone to have less in their life is crazy. There is more than enough abundance in this world for everyone. All we have to do is change our mindset and help each other to grow.

I recently watched the movie *MacFarland*. It is a true story about a California high school track team. It only took one person to change their history and their future. I recommend you watch it.

We all have the ability as adults to change our belief systems and raise our vibrations. At one time everyone believed that the world was flat. Yet Christopher Columbus took a ton of heat for his beliefs and proved them wrong. Funny thing was that the people who couldn't see it, still did not believe it and lived in fear. Sir Isaac Newton, Einstein, and many others had ideas and beliefs about things that had to be proved.

I have ideas, thoughts, and things that I need to prove for myself. I have learned that when I trust my gut, the proving's happen automatically.

Trusting your Gut

When I took the first picture, around four in the afternoon, I thought my camera had junk on the lens. I wiped the lens and took a few more photos. The orbs changed position; that was all. I had been writing an email to my office concerning a child who was very ill. I thought about a song that played on the radio after we had to put our beloved Portnoy, our family dog, to sleep. The name of the song was "When 10,000 Angels Cry." It came on the radio during my drive home in pouring rain as I left the veterinary hospital. I cried all the way home. That same song came over the speakers at the resort while I was writing my email. I thought of this child, I thought of our dog, and I asked for 10,000 angels to be by our side. I felt so sad. I got up from the desk in the room and walked onto the patio to look down on the beach so I could find my husband. I saw sparkles of light in the air and decided to go get my camera. I took many photos over the next several hours. There was little to no wind, no precipitation, just a beautiful sun, a few clouds, and my friends. The next thing I heard was the song "In the Arms of an Angel" by Sarah McLachlan. I now understood the message. I sat back down at my computer and finished my email response as to what to do for this little one. I then sat for a long while, contemplating coincidence or divine intervention. Divine intervention reminded me just how painful situations can be, and just how comforting a kind word, help, information, or instruction can be as well. My email reflected my experience and my advice for the parents. It was heartfelt and appropriate. A few weeks later I received a response from the father, a two-page email. He said how much my email had affected him, how much better his child was, and he thanked me. At first I felt uncomfortable. Then, after meditating, reflecting on his email…I got it. My intention of healing extended to him. My openness and wanting to have God heal his family and his child, went directly into all of them. Isn't that what this is all about?

Trusting your gut instinct is very important. It is as easy as a child choosing the color of a crayon. They just instinctively know the right color to use. They may hesitate a few moments, but then they grab the perfect crayon to finish their coloring project. Then it is perfect.

As we become adults we seem to find it more and more difficult to make decisions or trust our gut. We have spent years building up reasons to say "no." We have learned to go with the safe choice. A safe choice is fine, but I have found that "failing forward," taking a risk, and following my intuition actually produces more joy and satisfaction in the end.

My husband and I were traveling in Egypt a few years back. We traveled through Cairo, Sharm el-Sheikh, Aswan, Abu Simbel, Luxor, and Mt. Sinai. We were at the base of the Great Pyramid early one morning. I asked General Habib if we could go in to see the King's

Chapter 9 Putting It All Together

Chamber. He laughed and said sure. My gut said yes, but my brain said no way. I couldn't believe I was thinking this was a good idea. No way to turn back now. My poor husband and I crawled, duck-walked, and climbed through the narrow passageways for what seemed like an eternity. It was dark, and I thought to myself that there would be no way to rescue us if something happened. Halfway to the chamber my heart really started beating. I felt like I was starting to have a panic attack in that tight, dark tunnel.

I refocused my brain and realized that short of a nuclear disaster that morning, the pyramid was not going to collapse on us and we would probably be fine. So, we continued to crawl, duck-walk, and climb the small wooden ladders in the tunnel. All of a sudden I could see "light at the end of the tunnel." Now I know why people say that phrase....because you are so fricking happy to see the light, and I was. The chamber had an opening at the top of the stone to let a small amount of light through. What an excellent design--no lightbulbs needed here! I told my husband that we had to kiss in the middle of the chamber under the light shining in. He happily obliged. I couldn't believe we'd made it; job well done.

I decided to sit down for a moment and take it all in. I sat on

the edge of what remained of the sarcophagus. Little did I know that I would read a book a few years later, describing the exact sarcophagus and that Jesus may have been in the same place many, many years ago. The enormity of the experience is hard to describe. Spiritual, exhilarating, scary, and awe-inspiring. I felt so insignificant and blessed, considering the grand scheme of the world. Had I not trusted my gut intuition that I would be fine if I crawled into the Great Pyramid, I would have missed one of the most amazing events that needed to happen in my life. Thank you to God, and thank you to the angels looking after us.

I can also tell you that sliding and crawling out of the Great Pyramid went much faster than getting in. Got to love gravity and superhuman motivation to get back out again!

10 FOCUSED INTENTION

I wrote this book from a place of *love* and with *Focused Intention*. My goal was to write it in a style that would help you remember the tools and techniques you can use to heal yourself. After reading a book or watching a movie we mostly remember a specific scene or comment, like "Say hello to my little friend" from the move *Scarface* or "Give my daughter the medicine" from *Terms of Endearment*.

We generally do not remember all of the details of a book or a movie - just the things that impacted us and made us feel it in our body, see it in our mind, scared the crap out of us, made us cry, or caused us to think about that "thing" long after the movie was over or the book was finished. We don't store or retain a bullet list of "Do It Now, One Hundred Steps To Change Your Life." Well, I don't remember that kind of stuff. I remember things because of how they made me feel: "Oh, wow, that is so cool, I want to try it, do it, see it, etc." We proceed to explore this "new thing" because we had a gut feeling about it. We try something small and new, and then that turns into something big and familiar. Babies are not born with the skills to be an Indy racecar driver on their first day on Earth. They have to grow, learn, practice, and then perfect their skills. Babies take things one step at a time, one day at a time. Then all of a sudden they are thirty years old and holding a trophy at the Indy 500. I believe this is what life is about--learning something new every day and sharing those skills to improve our lives and the lives of others.

Throughout my life small things and big things have changed my "lone wolf's" path. Seeing "sparklers" in the air, hearing my name whispered with no one around, knowing things I could not possibly have known, helped me understand I was not alone in this world. My salamander Sam and his death by my hands was my first hard lesson about life and death, and that my actions could have changed the outcome.

For every tough earthly lesson I have completed, heaven has given me another opportunity to grow and learn about the things we cannot see, and to share with you that heavenly help is available to all of us, just for the asking. The ability to read at lightning speed and retain massive amounts of information on how to heal the human body is also a gift from heaven. Being able to channel healing messages from Spirit and crossed-over loved ones to those still living, *priceless*. I so look forward to my "follow-up lessons," as there will always be a silver lining to share.

I believe everyone needs a little loving "nudge" sometimes. I want to "nudge" you with heaven's help, educate you, expand your understanding of our three-dimensional life, make you laugh, make you reflect, and help you advance on your soul's incredible journey, with minimal "smackdowns." My job is to spark that "knowingness" within you and to encourage you to ask for Heaven's intervention. My goal is to share what I have learned and experienced so that with just a little bit of *focused intention*, you can start to heal yourself and your loved ones.

I hope to forever embed in your Mind, Body, and Spirit, that anything is possible. All we have to do is ask.

FOCUSED INTENTION

Faith in things that we cannot see.
Optimism in the outcome.
Courage to do the right thing.
Understanding of others despair.
Selflessness and compassion for others and ourselves.
Enlightenment arises when we have faith.
Dream and it becomes possible.

Integrity in all that we do.
Nurture yourself and others.
Trust your intuition.
Educate yourself on what you believe to be impossible.
New behavior will change the outcome.
Transformation happens, just like a caterpillar turning into a butterfly.
Invest your time in meditation, prayer, and gratitude.
Opportunity happens when we ask Heaven for intervention.
Namaste – the Spirit within me honors and respects the Spirit within you, or, in my words, "the Divine in me, wishes you, health, happiness, and love, in every way."

Chapter 10 Focused Intention

> May the longtime Sun shine upon you,
> All love surround you,
> And the pure light within you,
> Guide your way on.

Mike Heron, Incredible String Band, 1968

ABOUT THE AUTHOR

Diana Alba is a traditional naturopath, classical homeopath, certified thermographer, qEEG and brain neurointegration specialist, nutritional consultant, reiki master, artist, author, psychic medium, wife, mother, and owner of Pristine Health, A Natural Choice, located in Denver, Colorado. She has helped thousands of people for the past twenty years to heal their mind, body, and spirit. Her goal is to teach you, educate you, heal you, share messages from spirit, and then set you free with the tools to heal yourself. When she is not with clients, she is most likely reading the latest scientific journals on health and healing, painting, photographing angels, orbs, and spirit, or frightening her husband and their two mischievous dogs. You can visit her at www.dianaalba.com.

ACKNOWLEDGEMENTS

I would like to recognize everyone who has crossed my path so far on this journey called life. Without the experiences I have had, the opportunities I have been given, the intense pain I have felt or witnessed, and the immense joy and love I have been graced with, I simply would not have much to talk about.

I want to thank my dear friend Cari Gallo, the best real-estate agent in Denver, for giving me the most beautiful angel statue. I named this angel "Mary." Such a wonderful daily reminder of how blessed I am.

I would like to acknowledge and lovingly thank Amanda Sarkisian (my youngest daughter) for her incredible strength and her photos of Archangel Chamuel, whose beauty graces the cover of this book.

Mary's Angel, zooming by her feet.

Another beautiful Colorado evening with a friend.

www.ingramcontent.com/pod-product-compliance
Lightning Source LLC
Chambersburg PA
CBHW041608220426
43667CB00001B/4